Hearing the Word of God

Reflections on the Sunday Readings
Year A

John R. Donahue, S.J.

LITURGICAL PRESS
Collegeville, Minnesota

www.litpress.org

Excerpts from the *New American Bible with Revised New Testament and Psalms* © 1991, 1986, 1970 Confraternity of Christian Doctrine, Inc., Washington, DC. Used with permission. All rights reserved. No portion of the *New American Bible* may be reprinted without permission in writing from the copyright holder.

Excerpts from the *Lectionary for Mass for Use in the Dioceses of the United States of America, second typical edition* © 1970, 1986, 1992, 1998, 2001 Confraternity of Christian Doctrine, Inc., Washington, DC. All rights reserved. No part of the *Lectionary for Mass* may be reproduced by any means without permission in writing from the copyright owner.

Year A: ISBN 0-8146-2785-4
Year B: ISBN 0-8146-2783-8
Year C: ISBN 0-8146-2784-6

1	2	3	4	5	6	7	8	9

Library of Congress Cataloging-in-Publication Data

Donahue, John R.
    Hearing the word of God : reflections on the Sunday readings : year A / John R. Donahue.
        p. cm.
    Includes bibliographical references.
    ISBN 0-8146-2785-4 (pbk. : alk. paper)
    1. Bible—Meditations. 2. Catholic Church. Lectionary for Mass (U.S.). Year A. 3. Catholic Church—Prayer-books and devotions—English. I. Title.

BS491.5.D65 2004
242'.3—dc22

2004006463

Contents

Calendar for 2004–2005

Introduction

On December 4, 2003, the Church celebrated the fortieth anniversary of the promulgation of the Constitution on the Sacred Liturgy *(Sacrosanctum Concilium)* by the Second Vatican Council (1962–1965), and on November 18, 2005, the Church will commemorate the fortieth anniversary of the promulgation of the Dogmatic Constitution on Divine Revelation *(Dei Verbum)*. These documents, which span the history of the council, brought to fruition two of the major renewal movements of the twentieth century. In the four decades since the council, they have been major factors in the renewal of Church life and preaching.

The Constitution on the Liturgy mandated: "In sacred celebrations a more ample, more varied, and more suitable reading from sacred scripture should be restored" and "The ministry of preaching is to be fulfilled most faithfully and carefully. The sermon, moreover, should draw its content mainly from scriptural and liturgical sources" (no. 34). The constitution stressed the vital role of the scriptural homily for every liturgical celebration. The Dogmatic Constitution on Divine Revelation stressed the primacy of Scripture in all aspects of Church life, and in almost verbal agreement with the Constitution on the Liturgy stated:

> The Church has always venerated the Scriptures just as she venerates the body of the Lord, since, especially in sacred liturgy, she unceasingly receives and offers to the faithful the bread of life from the table both of God's Word and of Christ's Body (no. 21; see the Constitution on the Sacred Liturgy, no. 48).

The faith and life of countless people today are nurtured by thoughtful and well-prepared biblical homilies, and lay people and clergy continue to crowd workshops, institutes, and study days devoted to Scripture. The Catholic community is becoming a Bible-reading, Bible-praying Church. Yet, countermovements are emerging as Sunday after Sunday "agenda" preaching is recommended or mandated, for example, preaching on vocations, on missions, and even on liturgical regulations, often in tension with the prescribed Lectionary readings. A growing number of often-younger preachers draw primarily on the Catechism of the

Catholic Church or on magisterial documents for their homilies. Still valid and in force, however, is the mandate of the Second Vatican Council for biblical preaching, and the pilgrim Church, even apart from the mandate, is sustained by the table of God's Word and Christ's Body. The Church is continually summoned to "renew the renewal."

These reflections on the Sunday readings first appeared in *America* magazine from Advent 2001 through the Solemnity of Christ the King 2002. This was a time a great sadness in the Church in the United States, precipitated by the revelations in January 2002 of sexual abuse by clergy and a history of evasion and cover-ups by the hierarchy. Even as I write these comments two years later, there are hints of further doleful revelations, and the impact of the scandal on the lives of millions of faithful Catholics is yet to be measured. The reflections on the Sunday readings here could not but help reflect the impact of these events. I have altered them in places when they were too time-conditioned, but did not want to omit them totally. Proclaiming the Scripture involves a double "hearing": listening to the Word of God and attentiveness to the hearers of the Word.

In giving lectures and workshops over the years to groups of lay people, religious, and priests, I have suggested that we should always find the good news in a particular Sunday gospel in the context of the whole Gospel. There is a rhythm of interpretation where the richness of a particular passage is enhanced by the theology of the whole Gospel, while simultaneously shaping that theology. To preach or even reflect upon any particular section of Matthew (Year A), a person should be immersed in the theology and literary quality of the larger Gospel. I have included a short appendix of works that will hopefully contribute to an enriched engagement with Matthew and allow the readers to grow in appreciation of the work of the scribe trained for the kingdom of heaven who "brings from his storehouse both the new and the old" (Matt 13:52).

This volume concludes the revised versions of the reflections written originally as "The Word" for *America* magazine, as I stated above. As previously, I owe much gratitude to Fr. Thomas Reese, s.j., for inviting me to write the column, and especially to Fr. Robert Collins, s.j., for his weekly editing and helpful suggestions. I also am most appreciative for the work of the editors at the Liturgical Press, not simply on my volume but because of their immense contributions to biblical studies and theology. Above all, I thank the original readers for their interest and comments both critical and appreciative, and apologize for not always responding to them. May God's word continue to be a light to your paths (Ps 118:105).

John R. Donahue, s.j.
Ignatius House
Baltimore, Maryland

First Sunday of Advent

Readings: Isa 2:1-5; Ps 122:1-2, 3-4, 4-5, 6-7, 8-9; Rom 13:11-14; Matt 24:37-44

**"Because of my relatives and friends,
I will say 'Peace be within you!'" (Ps 122:8).**

WAITING IN FAITH AND HOPE

Life today often seems like a brief interlude between rushing and waiting. We rush to airports only to wait in line, hurry off to Christmas sales (or returns) and again wait, and even stand in long lines to receive the Eucharist. Waiting involves a necessary slowing down as well as hope of fulfillment.

The Advent season that begins the Church year summons us to slow down, even at a rather hectic time, but also to live in expectation of the various "arrivals" of Christ: his future arrival at the consummation of history (today's gospel), his coming as a human like us in history, and his continuing entry into our personal history. Through ritual and readings the Church sacramentalizes our waiting over the next weeks and sets before us three figures of expectation as models: the prophet Isaiah, John the Baptist, and Mary.

During this Advent especially, I recommend a deeper engagement with Isaiah, not simply through the liturgical readings but through Bible study and prayer. The book of Isaiah spans the period from the rise of the Assyrian empire in 745 B.C., through Sennacherib's siege of Jerusalem (701 B.C., Isaiah 1–39), when "the Assyrian came down like the wolf on the fold" (Lord Byron), to the Babylonian empire, the Exile (587–537), the return under Cyrus, the Lord's "anointed" (Isaiah 40–55), and the hope for a time when all nations will stream to Zion (Isaiah 56–66).

Though the work of many hands, theological themes first forged by Isaiah of Jerusalem (Isaiah 1–39), in times more tumultuous than our recent history, permeate the whole work. All the first readings this Advent of Year A contain visions of hope found in the early movements of this oratorio. In an exceptional commentary (*Isaiah 1–39*, 1998), Walter Brueggemann compares Isaiah to "a mighty oratorio whereby Israel sings its story of faith." Sounding through this oratorio are paeans of the utter holiness of God, God's anger at the infidelity of the people through injustice and reliance on worldly power, always, however, counterpointed by a call for change of heart:

> Put away your misdeeds from before my eyes;
>> cease doing evil; learn to do good. Make justice your aim . . . .
>
> Though your sins be like scarlet,
>> they may become white as snow (Isa 1:16-18).

Today's reading follows closely the initial chapter, in which Isaiah bitterly indicts sin and summons people to repent. It comprises an oracle that gives hope for a time in the future when the people will proclaim a message of justice and a time when violence will cease:

> They shall beat their swords into plowshares
>> and their spears into pruning hooks (Isa 2:4).

War and preparing for war will cease. The holy God is repelled by injustice and violence and summons people to turn to a different course. How unrealistic the vision of Isaiah seems, especially during this Advent when violence and war prevail! Yet Isaiah's messages were proclaimed in a no less difficult time, when the nation was threatened with destruction.

Do we all not need new images of hope today? Years ago, in a stunning little book, *Images of Hope,* William Lynch, S.J., noted that people in sorrow or depression suffer an impoverishment of imagination. They simply cannot imagine a world different from the one in which they are locked. The critic Hugh Kenner once wrote: "Whoever can give his people better stories than the ones they live by is like the priest in whose hands common bread and wine become capable of feeding the very soul and he may think of forging in some invisible smithy the uncreated conscience of his race" (*The Pound Era).*

Advent reminds all of us that we are people who can hope against hope (Rom 4:18) and who are not submerged by a culture of fear dinned over the video screens. Christians are to be a prophetic people who can dream of new, perhaps unheard of paths toward peace and reconciliation. Groups with the names "Plowshares," "Pax Christi" and "Fellowship of Reconciliation" raise banners of peace, not war. As a priestly people we are summoned to tell people better stories than those they live by. In the midst of struggle and doubt, Isaiah did just that. As we feed our souls in the Eucharist this Advent, can we envision ways to forge the yet "uncreated conscience" of people today?

PRAYING WITH SCRIPTURE

- Begin to read Isaiah prayerfully, perhaps for ten minutes each day of Advent, letting his words refresh your weary heart.

- Pray for peace, not simply amid the present conflict but for a more enduring peace, when "justice will bring about peace; right will produce calm and security" (Isa 32:17).

- Think of ways that you can bring images of hope to others "waiting in line."

Second Sunday of Advent

Readings: Isa 11:1-10; Ps 72:1-2, 7-8, 12-13, 17; Rom 15:4-9; Matt 3:1-12

"Justice shall flower in his days, and profound peace, till the moon be no more" (Ps 72:7).

DINING WITH WOLF AND LAMB

Another year winds down. The days grow ever shorter, and Advent seems especially gray, a time "When yellow leaves, or none, or few, do hang / Upon those boughs which shake against the cold, / Bare ruin'd choirs, where late the sweet birds sang" (Shakespeare, *Sonnet 73*). Despite exhortations and efforts to get on with life as usual, it is difficult to be people of hope when our consciousness is flooded with one warning or dire prediction after another. And yet it was in a period just like this that Isaiah forged the beautiful poem of messianic hope in today's first reading. This section of Isaiah follows immediately the vivid description of Sennacherib's invasion: "Ramah is in terror, Gibeah of Saul has fled" (Isa 10:29). Isaiah rejoices that through God's saving help, the invasion was halted at the walls of Jerusalem: "He will shake his fist at the mount of daughter Zion" (10:32). Assyrian chronicles give a far different picture, in which Sennacherib shuts up Hezekiah in Jerusalem, like a bird in a cage.

More striking, then, is Isaiah's paean of hope for a just king from the house of David. This king will be enveloped by God's Spirit and endowed with wisdom, understanding, and other virtues necessary to lead God's people. Leadership will be expressed in judging the poor with justice. Biblical judging always has the overtone of protection (see the book of Judges), and a major theme of Isaiah and other prophets is that the justice of king and nation is measured on the scale of concern for the vulnerable in society (see Psalm 72, a virtual job description of the king). This king will not be clothed with weapons of war, but with justice around his waist and faithfulness a belt upon his hips.

In the middle of this oracle of promise, the atmosphere shifts. Justice in the land will affect even the animal creation. In startling metaphors of peace between natural enemies, Isaiah images qualities that produce justice and peace among humans: welcome (the wolf will be a guest of the lamb), rest and harmony, concluding with an amazing image of innocence and vulnerability: the child not being harmed by the ancient symbol of evil, the snake.

Is this just beautiful poetry that inspired Handel's *Messiah,* or can the poet of 2,700 years ago speak to us as well? The theory of government envisioned by Isaiah is a prophetic voice for us today. The "option for the poor" is muted by a penchant for the prosperous. This option means that socioeconomic practices and decisions must be assessed by their impact on the most vulnerable members of society. Isaiah's vision flies in the face of political power today, which most often is in the hands of the wealthy and powerful and used for their own benefit (see Walter Brueggemann, *Isaiah*).

John the Baptist, another Advent figure of expectation, is also a prophet, but today he thunders judgment against the contented and powerful, pointing to a stronger one who will not preach a baptism (cleansing) leading to repentance but will preach with the Holy Spirit and fire. John's Jesus will be a threatening figure who will winnow the good from the bad and throw evildoers (the chaff) into the fire. Yet John was disappointed, or rather his hope was transformed. Jesus was not the fiery reformer John limned, but rather one who ate with tax collectors and sinners and warned against a hurried separation of the wheat and chaff (Matt 13:24-30).

Isaiah's vision and John's prophecy were not fulfilled in the way they expected. They lived in hope and died in faith. Despite eloquent teaching on social justice by Pope John Paul II and local bishops' conferences, the light of hope for "the land's afflicted" throughout the world seems dimmer day by day. Isaiah hoped for the gifts of the Spirit that would create a new kind of king who would be "a signal for the nations" (11:10). John points to a mighty one who will baptize and renew people with God's spirit. We will conclude Advent with a young woman overshadowed by the Spirit, destined to give birth to that heir of David whose message, once heard and authentically lived, offers hope in this bittersweet season of joy and sadness.

PRAYING WITH SCRIPTURE

- Pray with Isaiah and form images of peace and reconciliation that would apply today.

- Pray for political leaders, that they may realize that power should be at the service of justice.
- Paul exhorts his community to welcome one another as Christ has welcomed them (Rom 15:7). Pray about ways that Advent-Christmas can be a season of welcome.

The Immaculate Conception
of the Blessed Virgin Mary

Readings: Gen 3:9-15, 20; Ps 98:1, 2-3, 3-4; Eph 1:3-6, 11-12;
Luke 1:26-38

"Hail, full of grace, the Lord is with you" (Luke 1:28).

FOREVER GRACED!

Though Mary's freedom from sin was widely proclaimed in the early
Church, especially by the Greek patristic writers, and the U.S. bishops
had chosen Mary as patron of this land under the title of the Immacu-
late Conception (1847), the formal feast dates from the declaration made
by Pope Pius IX on December 8, 1854, that Mary "from the first moment of her conception was, by the singular grace and privilege of God
and the merits of Jesus Christ, the Savior of the human race, was pre-
served from all stain of sin."

While in popular piety this feast is often confused with the virgin
birth of Jesus, which the gospel announces, the feast does not suggest
that Mary was herself conceived in any miraculous manner. The greeting of Gabriel that Mary is a recipient of God's favor and gracious love,
"full of grace," captures the meaning of the feast. Mary is one who does
not turn away from God (Thomas Aquinas's definition of sin) but is totally open to God's love, captured in her final words: "I am the hand-
maid of the Lord. May it be done to me according to your word."

We live in a world where sin and evil seem to reign supreme, yet the
readings offer a different vision. The first reading, from Genesis, tells us
that the human race is flawed because our first parents turned away
from the gifts of God, yet it proclaims a message of hope: "the woman"
will strike the head of the serpent. Traditional exegesis views Mary as
the new Eve who will mediate the victory over evil. More importantly,
the feast counters the ancient myth that somehow woman is evil, by affirming that a woman's body is suffused with holiness.

The reading from Ephesians proclaims that all Christians are chosen
to be "holy and without blemish" and that "in love he [God] has destined

us for adoption to himself through Jesus Christ" (3:4-5). The gap between Mary, the sinless one, and the baptized Christian is narrowed. The fullness of God's grace and love that embraces Mary from the first moment of her existence is to touch every Christian Love and grace, not sin, are to crown their lives as they did the life of Mary.

While celebrating the unique sinlessness of Mary, the feast should not detract from Mary's humanity. A senior Sister of Mercy once remarked that one of the most frightening verses in the Gospels occurs after Mary commits herself fully to God's will, when "the angel departed from her" (Luke 1:38). Nowhere else in the Gospel does a divine messenger assure Mary of God's presence. Her son will be a sign of contradiction, and a sword will pierce her heart (Luke 2:34-35); she is puzzled by his mission and actions (Luke 2:48; Mark 3:31; John 2:4); she will suffer the horrible pain of a mother watching a brutal execution (John 19:25-27).

Often people today in the midst of intense suffering or a family tragedy, such as the loss of a child, feel that God has abandoned them, with a haunting sense that they bear the guilt for what has happened. Yet Mary, ever sinless, whose life was a constant "yes" to God's will, bore the pains of the human condition. In the words of the ancient litany, she who is *mater divinae gratiae* ("mother of divine grace") is also *refugium peccatorum* and *consolatrix afflictorum* ("refuge of sinners" and "comforter of the afflicted").

PRAYING WITH SCRIPTURE:

• Pray quietly the Hail Mary, pausing over those words that bring Mary into your life.

• Repeat the phrase from the opening prayer of today's liturgy: "Trace in our actions the lines of her love, in our hearts the readiness of her faith."

• Repeat prayerfully the words of the angel as addressed to yourself: "Do not be afraid, Mary, for you have found favor with God."

Third Sunday of Advent

Readings: Isa 35:1-6a, 10; Ps 146:6-7, 8-9, 9-10; Jas 5:7-10; Matt 11:2-11

"Say to those whose hearts are frightened: Be strong, fear not!" (Isa 35:4).

VOICE FROM A GALILEAN JAIL!

Resonating through the readings today are messages of hope for people almost three millennia ago, for people at the beginning of the first millennium, and for people today. Amidst the turmoil of internal injustice and invasion by the Assyrians, Isaiah proclaims: "Be strong, fear not! Here is your God, he comes with vindication . . . he comes to save you." James exhorts his community to faithful waiting (patience) for the coming of the Lord, and an imprisoned John the Baptist wonders whether his life's hope is to be fulfilled, "Are you the one who is to come or should we look for another?"

Especially powerful and poignant is the picture of John, the second figure of expectation for Advent. John, the spirit-possessed prophet who, like Amos and Isaiah, castigated the religious leaders of his day, proclaimed the coming wrath of God, and pointed to one coming even stronger than he, sits now in Herod Antipas's prison awaiting death, because he confronted with God's word the powerful and violent people of his day. John wonders if his life was worthwhile and asks his disciples to go to Jesus and ask if he really is the awaited stronger one.

Jesus' answer is as much a challenge to John as is his life to us today. Jesus is not the stronger one who will usher in the day of wrath and winnow the wheat and the chaff, but the one whose deeds gather up the most profound hopes of Isaiah: the blind see the beauty of a dawn; the deaf hear the song of the birds; the lame jump up; lepers rejoin their families; the poor receive good news that God is on their side (Isa 26:19; 29:18-19; 35:6; 61:1). John, who lived proclaiming God's word, must now wait for death sustained by faith and hope in that word.

John is for us a symbol of hopes proclaimed and hopes transformed. A great challenge of faith today is to offer Church and world visions of a renewed and transformed world, without seeing the fruit of our efforts. When I think of John, I think of parents holding infants at baptism, rapt in love and in expectation that these little children will share and form a future that those who gave them life will not ultimately see. With John they prepare the way, but the unfolding of this way is often vastly different from their expectation. Not to give up on the present in the face of a threatening and uncertain future caused Jesus to say that "among those born of women there has been none greater than John the Baptist; yet the least in the kingdom of heaven is greater than he" (Matt 11:11).

The heart of Matthew's community and of our churches today are the "little ones," not the powerful in fine clothes and royal palaces. They are the poor and the mourners and those who hunger for justice. Often, with "little faith," they worry about what they will eat and what they will wear, and find it difficult to hear Jesus' reassuring words, "Seek first the kingdom of God and his righteousness, and all these things will be given you besides" (Matt 6:33). Like Peter when he was about to be swallowed by waves, they cry out, "Lord, save us! We are perishing!" (Matt 8:25). But this little faith, the size of a mustard seed, is enough to tell mountains to get moving and "nothing will be impossible for you" (Matt 17:20).

Advent is a time that reminds us that even with little or shaken faith, we can foster great hopes and plant those seeds that may blossom into a future that we, like John, may never see. Today parents, teachers, people working for justice and peace, priests and religious living and speaking God's word, along with those burdened by illness while praying for the world's healing—all are messengers coming before Christ and preparing the way. Preparing for the future, living with faith and dying in hope was John's calling. We who are privileged to be but the least in God's kingdom have a mission no less august, while no less daunting.

PRAYING WITH SCRIPTURE

- Place yourself with John in prison, questioning whether the Jesus he foretold is the one who is actually present. Ask how John's question speaks to you today.

- In prayer and gratitude, remember those little ones who have been greatest in the kingdom of heaven.

- In prayer, dream of a future for those for whom you are preparing the way.

Fourth Sunday of Advent

Readings: Isa 7:1-14; Ps 24:1-2, 3-4, 5-6; Rom 1:1-17; Matt 1:18-24

**"Joseph, son of David, do not be afraid
to take Mary your wife into your home" (Matt 1:20).**

A Real "Holy Joe"

As the celebration of the Incarnation nears, the readings echo with wonder and joy. Amid virtual despair about the future of his kingdom, YHWH tells King Ahaz to ask for a sign, which he will not do, lest he tempt God. But Isaiah intervenes with an oracle of salvation. Life is affirmed at the doorstep of destruction: a virgin will bear a child, and his name shall signify his destiny—God will be with us. The solemn introduction to Romans (second reading) heralds the arrival of a descendant of David "according to the flesh," who was established as the "Son of God in power." The gospel portrays the message announced to Joseph that Mary, who was betrothed (that is, legally married) to Joseph, will bear a son with a double name: "Jesus," because he will save his people from their sins, and "Emmanuel" ("God is with us") in fulfillment of Isaiah's prophecy.

In liturgy, art, and devotion we rightly merge the infancy narratives of Matthew and Luke to create a Yuletide tapestry. Naturally, Mary, mother, and her child occupy center stage. Matthew, though has another dimension, which is important for our time. The central "human character" in Matthew is Joseph. In contrast to Luke, Joseph, not Mary, receives divine messages from angels—and in dreams. Mary is most often spoken *about* and initiates no action, while Joseph's obedience to God's word appears at every critical juncture. Faced with doubt over Mary's pregnancy, Joseph "did as the angel commanded him and took his wife into his home" (Matt 1:24).

After the birth of the child, Joseph again receives a dream revelation and takes the "child and his mother" to Egypt to avoid the murderous actions of Herod, and after a third dream vision returns the family to

11

Nazareth. In each case Joseph also is the human agent by which Scripture is fulfilled. Yet, though Matthew and Luke present independent infancy narratives, there is wonderful parallelism. Mary and Joseph react in similar ways to angelic messages. Both are told not to fear in face of a seemingly impossible future; both are told that the Holy Spirit has acted, and both are given a sign of God's presence. Throughout the narratives, both hear the word of God and act upon it.

In Christian art Joseph is often portrayed more like Jesus' grandfather or great-grandfather than parent. An example is a painting by Guido Reni (1635, in the Hermitage Museum in St. Petersburg), which shows Joseph with gray hair and beard, lovingly holding the infant, who plays with his beard. One beautiful exception is El Greco's Joseph, portrayed as a vigorous young man, with Jesus clinging to his legs; here Joseph is a figure of trust and protection. The historical Joseph, a carpenter or one who worked in stone, was most likely young and vigorous, excited about a future with a woman he so loved that he would not invoke a harsh law against supposed adultery, but still followed the law to put her away "quietly." Yet out of his shattered hopes would come forth one whom he would name Jesus and Emmanuel, "God with us."

Today, when parenting is both so challenging and so threatened, Joseph provides a wonderful image of a father. The future of his child unfolds in dreams. Even though he cannot see what the future holds, he protects and cares for his family in the face of murder and exile; he is faithful to God's word; he is called to a life of hard work, providing for the son Mary will bear, as well as the extended family of brothers and sisters of Jesus (Mark 3:32). When coupled with the Luke's portrait of Mary, Matthew's Joseph provides a model of complementarity for parents today as they engage in that most divine of tasks: bringing forth new life and guiding their sons and daughters along the way of Christ.

PRAYING WITH SCRIPTURE

- Young men about to marry might pray over how Joseph can be a model for them.

- Throughout the infancy narrative there constantly appears the divine command "Do not fear." Place before God in prayer those fears that overshadow your life.

- Matthew's Gospel begins with the presence of Emmanuel, "God with us" (1:23) and ends with a promise that Jesus will "be with" his followers until the end of time (28:20). Pray over ways that Jesus is with you during this Advent season.

The Nativity of the Lord (Christmas)

Readings: Isa 9:1-6; Ps 96:1-2, 2-3, 11-12, 13; Titus 2:11-14;
Luke 2:1-14 (Midnight Mass); Isa 62:11-12; Ps 97:1, 6, 11-12;
Titus 3:4-7; Luke 2:15-20 (Mass at Dawn); Isa 52:7-10; Ps 98:1,
2-3, 3-4, 5-6; Heb 1:1-6; John 1:1-18 (Mass During the Day)

> **"Your eternal Word has taken upon himself our**
> **human weakness,**
> **giving our mortal nature immortal value"**
> **(Preface of Christmas, III).**

GIFTS ABOUNDING

Because of the ancient custom of celebrating three distinct Christmas Masses, the liturgy offers a treasury of readings that bring out different aspects of the celebration. The first readings herald the messianic promises of Isaiah and the good news of salvation (Isa 52:7-10; 62:11-12), and the psalms echo Israel's royal enthronement rituals. The gospels for the Masses at midnight and dawn announce in rhythmic cadence Luke's story of the birth and initial revelation of Jesus, while John's poetic prologue (John 1:1-18) reaches beyond time to proclaim that the Word that was with God and was God has become flesh and has made his dwelling place among us.

Like a dazzling fireworks exhibit, the Christmas readings are almost too much to assimilate at one time. Everyone seems to have their favorite Christmas story and Christmas images, and yet all focus around the profound mystery that God's eternal Word has taken on human flesh. The human is the bearer of the divine as Jesus reveals the God who is our origin and destiny.

This Christ-event (the incarnation, life, death, and resurrection of Jesus, seen as one act of God) is heralded through the New Testament in forms as diverse as the cadences of the Philippians hymn (Phil 2:6-11), early creedal affirmations (Rom 1:1-2), missionary preaching (Acts 13:26-29), and cries of gratitude (Gal 2:19-21). Yet only in Matthew and Luke is the origin of this mystery proclaimed *in story*, in ways that constantly enrich our faith.

Matthew begins with a genealogy tracing Jesus' origin through saints and sinners and a series of extraordinary births, showing, as Zwingli once observed, the unmerited triumph of God's grace. Jesus is born into a world of homelessness and violence ("there was no room for them in the inn," Luke 2:7). A wondrous parade of people in Luke are touched by Jesus' coming: an aging priest and his childless wife; a young woman called to bring forth a child in a way unheard of in human history; the dark night sky shining with God's glory and shepherd boys hearing "good news of great joy"; an aging couple living and waiting for God's anointed. While in Matthew an anointed Jewish king turns out to be a brutal killer, wise men from afar follow a star to kneel before the child and his mother. Jesus begins his life an exile from land and people and returns to grow up in an obscure village.

The Christmas stories affirm humanity in all its glory and brokenness. They are retold not simply every Christmas, but in the lives of countless unnamed people among whom God's Word continues to become flesh and to dwell among us (John 1:14).

PRAYING WITH SCRIPTURE

- Amid the rush of preparation, parents should pause to think how they are really preparing for the coming of Christ to their children.

- As we celebrate the joy of the season, remember in prayer the victims of violence and tragic accidents.

- In this season of gift-giving, prayerfully list those gifts from God you have received the past year.

The Holy Family of Jesus, Mary, and Joseph

Readings: Sir 3:2-6, 12-14; Ps 128:1-2, 3, 4-5; Col 3:12-17 [21];
Matt 2:13-15, 19-23

"Rise, take the child and his mother, flee to Egypt" (Matt 2:13).

FAMILY VALUES

The readings of the Christmas cycle are like a large medieval tapestry on which we can follow the narrative sequence of the birth and infancy of Jesus or pause before one scene of particular beauty. The liturgical cycle does not proceed in linear fashion, since the celebration of the Holy Family and the flight to Egypt precedes the solemnity of Mary and naming of Jesus, while the cycle concludes with the visit of the Magi that precipitates the flight. Each narrative is a miniature of the mystery of God's sending his Son "born of a woman" so that we "might receive adoption" as sons and daughters (Gal 4:5).

The Holy Family could well be called the "Refugee Family." No sooner had the night visitors laid their gifts at the infant's feet than Joseph receives another command from God's messenger: "Rise, take the child and his mother, flee to Egypt." Scarcely on this earth, Jesus' future is determined by a brutal murderer, Herod the Great, who, after killing many members of his own family, would have little qualms about killing dozens of newborn children. How sadly contemporary such a picture is, when the anxious faces of refugee families from scenes of conflict throughout the world fill our TV screens.

Joseph's nighttime departure for Egypt, however frightening, is to fulfill God's plan to call his son out of Egypt, just as God's first love, Israel, was called forth from slavery and oppression in Egypt. Though Scripture tells us nothing about the sojourn of the family, their return plummets them into further danger from Herod's son, and they return to Nazareth, where now he who was heralded as Jesus, Savior, and "God

15

with us," is now simply a "Nazorean" (Matt 2:23), which later becomes a term of disdain used for Christians.

Suddenly the Christmas lights begin to dim. A holy family is not necessarily one secure from threatening dangers, not in the first century or today. The image of the flight of the Holy Family suggests today that the constant concern over family values must be joined to a struggle for the dignity and rights of every family.

The celebration of the Holy Family is joined closely to the octave of Christmas and the Solemnity of the Blessed Virgin Mary, the Mother of God, January 1 (not observed in 2005 as a holy day of obligation). Three themes echo through the readings: the gracious love of God manifest in the gift of "his Son," born of woman (Gal 4:4-7); Mary keeping (treasuring) these things in her heart; and the circumcision of Jesus (Luke 2:16-21).

After repeating the visit of the shepherds from the Christmas Mass at Dawn, the circumcision is narrated briefly. I remember from my childhood that only this section was read and welcomed as the shortest gospel of the year, appropriate for the day after New Year's Eve. To a very young child, the name of the feast had an aura of awe and mystery, especially when glancing at artwork showing Mary and the infant next to a religious official with a big knife.

The verb used for "keeping" or "treasuring" appears in Genesis 37:11 with the nuance of trying to fathom the deeper meaning of particular messages. Mary also "reflects" on them. Mary is not only one who physically gives birth to God's Son, but she continues to hear and ponder the meaning of God's word. As from the first moment of her appearance (Luke 1:26-38), Mary is the model disciple who hears and follows God's word, even amid uncertainty.

PRAYING WITH SCRIPTURE

- Pray over ways that your family and your parish may show concern for refugees and exiles.

- Paul tells the Colossians to "clothe themselves in love"—time to pray over a new wardrobe.

- As the Christmas season ends, list those things that you now treasure in your heart and ponder their meaning.

The Epiphany of the Lord

Readings: Isa 60:1-6; Ps 72:1-2, 7-8, 10-11, 12-13; Eph 3:2-3a, 5-6; Matt 2:1-12

"The Gentiles are coheirs, members of the same body, and copartners in the promise in Christ Jesus" (Eph 3:6).

STARSTRUCK!

The Epiphany, or manifestation of Jesus, is *the* Christmas feast among Eastern Christians, Orthodox or Uniate. The same readings are used for all three cycles and emphasize a number of themes. The first reading, from the final postexilic section of Isaiah, envisions the streaming of nations to a restored Jerusalem; the psalm heralds God's choice of a king who will manifest justice and peace to the nations and be concerned for the poor; and the gospel is the wonderful story of the sages (magi) from the East, who are led by a star (natural revelation) to come and worship the "newborn king of the Jews."

Jesus is a manifestation of God's grace (Eph 3:2) not simply for the people of the first covenant but for all nations. Christian iconography throughout history has captured this meaning as the magi became, first, three kings (from Psalm 72), but later, people of different age and color. The evolving traditions actualize an important theme of Matthew's Gospel. The visit of the magi anchors a great arch that extends to the final works of Jesus in the "Great Commission," where the risen Jesus sends forth the apostles to proclaim to all nations what he taught and did (28:16-20). Matthew's universalistic vision unfolds under this arch. At the Day of Judgment, those who voiced the proper confession of faith, "Lord, Lord," or worked miracles in the name of Jesus will be cast out with the ominous verdict "I never knew you," while those who do the will of "my Father in heaven" will be welcomed. When describing the mission of Jesus as servant, Matthew quotes fully Isaiah 42:1-4, where the servant "will proclaim justice to the Gentiles . . . and in his name the Gentiles will hope" (Matt 12:17-21). Most dramatically, those welcomed into paradise for caring for Jesus present in the least of his brothers and sisters are people who never explicitly recognized Jesus (Matt 25:31-46).

Matthew has special relevance in our present time. One of the greatest changes in the Catholic Church in the last quarter century has been its extraordinary growth in Africa, India, and throughout Asia. Religious pluralism is a fact, and our world needs celebrations of diversity more than uniformity. Like the wise people who came from the East bearing gifts to the newborn Christ, people from ancient and diverse cultures are bringing gifts to Christ's Body, the Church. At the same time, true inculturation of the gospel requires that we recognize the action of God already at work in other cultures.

Today's feast offers resources for continued reflection. The nations are led to either Jerusalem or Jesus by God and in God's good time. While affirming the centrality of Christ for salvation, the Church holds that explicit confession of Christ is not required. The magi came by ways unknown to us and were led by their own reading of signs in the heavens. When they returned "by another way," were their lives changed? Did they worship the newborn king of the Jews? The manifestations of God at this season are public; the ways people are drawn to him were and remain opaque to human eyes.

PRAYING WITH SCRIPTURE

• Look around your church on any given Sunday and pray in gratitude for its diversity.

• Pray over ways your parish or community might become more aware of the gifts that other cultures bring to the Church.

• Pray for the continuing progress of the dialogue between Roman Catholicism and the ancient Churches of the East.

The Baptism of the Lord

(First Sunday in Ordinary Time)

*Readings: Isa 42:1-4, 6-7; Ps 29:1-2, 3-4, 3, 9-10; Acts 10:34-38;
Matt 3:13-17*

**"Here is my servant whom I uphold,
my chosen one with whom I am pleased" (Isa 42:1).**

THE BEGINNING HOLDS THE FUTURE!

In the liturgy of the Church, the baptism of Jesus, along with the Epiphany and the wedding feast at Cana, form a triptych of public manifestations of Jesus. Though "baptism" suggests a ritual, the main themes of the readings are God's commissioning and manifestation of one who "establishes justice on the earth" (Isa 42:4).

The reading from Isaiah is the first of the four great "Servant Songs," (Isa 42:1-4; 49:1-6; 50:4-9; 52:13–53:12), which describe a figure who was chosen by God to proclaim justice through tenderness rather than force and who will ultimately be lifted up, not in triumph, but in shame and disgrace, giving his life as an offering for sin (Isa 53:12). Though Old Testament scholars debate the identity of the Servant—perhaps a prophet, a symbol of the suffering people, or a hoped-for royal figure—the application of these texts to Jesus forms one of the oldest theologies of the New Testament.

Matthew's baptism has distinctive characteristics. Only he recounts John's resistance: "I need to be baptized by you." This reflects the growing concern of Matthew's community to exalt Jesus over John (see 11:10-15), as well as to clarify that John's baptism was for sinners to symbolize repentance. Jesus states that his baptism is "to fulfill all righteousness," which is somewhat of an exegetical puzzle. "Righteousness" scarcely means observance of the Torah, since the Torah contains no prescript on baptism. A better translation would be "to bring to fullness all justice," which would envision Jesus as continuing the mission of the Servant (see Matt 12:15-21). Jesus is one who begins to show the way in which men and women will be made "right" or "just" before God and with fellow humans. This initial public appearance of Jesus prepares for the final heavenly assize, when people will be called "just" or "unjust" on the basis of their care of the suffering and marginal of the world (Matt 25:31-46).

Matthew emphasizes that in Jesus a new communication is opened between God and men and women. The heavens open, the Spirit descends like a dove hovering over the earth, recalling Genesis 1:2, and a voice from heaven resonant of the creative word in Genesis proclaims, "*This is* my beloved Son." In Mark and Luke the voice proclaims, "*You are* my beloved Son." In Mark the voice is heard only by Jesus, while Matthew alone stresses the public character of the baptism, so a Markan adoption is turned into a public inaugural commissioning.

In light of Jesus' final mandate to his disciples to "baptize all nations," early Christian interpreters quickly viewed Jesus' baptism as prefiguring their baptism. Today we should recall that baptism is both adoption into the very life of God and a mission to proclaim justice in the land, to be a light for the nations, to open the eyes of the blind, and to free prisoners from their dungeons (Isa 42:7). What an awesome task for a little baby—but not really for him or her, but rather for those who bring the child to baptism and are commissioned to renew their life of faith and to form their "beloved" son and daughter, so that they too may work to bring justice to its fullness.

PRAYING WITH SCRIPTURE

- As one baptized into Christ (Rom 6:3), think of the voice from heaven as addressed to you: "This is my beloved, in whom I am well pleased."

- In prayer recall that your baptism is a commission to "bring forth justice to the nations."

- Pray over ways in which you may be a public witness to the teaching of Christ.

Second Sunday in Ordinary Time

Readings: Isa 49:3, 5-6; Ps 40:2, 4, 7-8, 8-9, 10; 1 Cor 1:1-3; John 1:29-34

> **"Now I have seen and testified that he is the Son of God" (John 1:34).**

CALLED TO BE A WITNESS FOR THE DEFENSE

The period between the end of the Advent-Christmas-Epiphany cycle and Lent constitutes a brief return to "Ordinary Time." The initial events of the public life of Jesus continue the theme of the manifestation of Jesus by John the Baptist's witness of Jesus. The readings are united around the theme of vocation, which prepares for the narratives of the call and initial formation of the disciples on the coming Sundays. The Old Testament reading presents another Servant Song of Isaiah, in which God commissions the Servant to be a light to the nations, and the initial verses of 1 Corinthians recount Paul's call to be "an apostle of Christ Jesus."

Though the Baptist is the herald of Jesus' arrival in all the Gospels, his altered role in John reflects the Gospel's distinct theology. Three times in the prologue (John 1:7, 8, 15) John's role is to offer testimony about Jesus, which is completed by his final words in the Gospel (3:22-30). John's Gospel also makes clear that the Baptist is subordinate to Jesus: he is not the light; the one who comes "ranks ahead of me because he was before me." And although John speaks of Jesus' baptism, he does not actually baptize Jesus. John's farewell is "he must increase; I must decrease."

In John's Gospel the Baptist appears as a witness for the defense who offers true testimony about Jesus. Only in John does he call Jesus "the Lamb of God." "Lamb" is a tensive symbol, that is, one with multiple evocations rather than a single referent. It evokes Jesus as the Servant, who like a silent lamb is led to death in Isaiah 53:7 (see also Acts 8:32) or perhaps the paschal lamb sacrificed for the sin of the world (2 Cor 5:7). A less obvious but more cogent allusion may be the apocalyptic lamb in later Jewish tradition that overcomes evil beasts and crushes them (*Testament of Joseph,* 19:8; see Rev 7:17; 17:14) and that "by grace will save all the Gentiles and Israel" (*Testament of Joseph,* 19:11). The Baptist does not describe the mission of the Lamb as taking away sins (plural) but "the world's sin." In John sin is a power arrayed against Jesus, and "world" is often used negatively to depict the organized power of evil. A contemporary parallel would be structural or social sin.

One of the major themes of John's Gospel is that Jesus is "on trial" by worldly powers arrayed against him. This culminates in the long narrative of the trial of Jesus before Pilate, who represents worldly power and arrogance, which is "the sin of the world." By his example of service and love, Jesus conquers or takes away this sin, much as the apocalyptic lamb conquers evil beasts. This Lamb to whom the Baptist points will tell his followers that although they too will be hated by the world (John 15:18-19), they should have confidence because he has "conquered the world" (John 16:33).

Today's gospel is both a preview of Johannine theology and a summons to faithful witness. Despite the vocation of the Christian to find God's "footsteps" in the world, worldly powers and values are often in conflict with Christ's teachings. Being a witness for the defense today involves speaking the truth about Christ, but always with the attitude that "he must increase; I must decrease."

PRAYING WITH SCRIPTURE

- Soberly pray over that "sin of the world" that is manifest today in the arrogance of power.

- When your hear the term "Lamb of God" before receiving the Eucharist, think of the victory over evil promised in Christ.

- Pray over how you have been a witness to Christ amid various "trials."

Third Sunday in Ordinary Time

Readings: Isa 8:23–9:3; Ps 27:1, 4, 13-14; 1 Cor 1:10-13, 17; Matt 4:12-17 [23]

> **"The Lord is my life's refuge;**
> **of whom should I be afraid?" (Ps 27:1).**

KEYNOTING DISCIPLESHIP!

"She would have been a good woman," The Misfit said, "if it had been somebody there to shoot her every day of her life." So Flannery O'Connor's celebrated story "A Good Man Is Hard to Find." Like the Old Testament prophets and the parables of Jesus, O'Connor's often grotesque stories shock readers into seeing reality in a new way. The story begins simply, "The grandmother didn't want to go to Florida," and recounts the car trip that is detoured by the grandmother, waking from a nap at Toomsboro and promising the children a visit to an old plantation with secret panels. The reluctant father agrees and takes a detour, but the car crashes and turns over on a winding dirt road. The narrative moves from the comic to the tragic. A trio of escaped convicts led by "The Misfit" come along and proceed to murder the family (offstage as in a Greek tragedy). As she realizes that death looms, the grandmother becomes kind and compassionate, finally saying to The Misfit, "Why you're one of my babies. You're one of my own children!" Without a word the Misfit shoots her and praises her as a good woman.

Jesus' saying "Repent, for the kingdom of heaven is at hand" carries the same urgency. The way God rules, or is about to be revealed in Jesus, presents a life-and-death situation that causes people to reconsider their lives. This initial proclamation of Jesus anchors one part of an arch that extends to Jesus' concluding discourse to his disciples. The master returns suddenly to punish carousing servants (Matt 25:41-51); the ten bridesmaids don't have time to buy oil to replenish their lamps and hear the ominous words, "I do not know you." The beginning and end of the gospel herald the crisis brought by the presence of God's reign and warning that "it may be too late!"

Repentance today is not simply an emotion of sorrow but taking a second look at our lives. As appalling as the murder of innocent people in recent months has been, and as ghastly as the murders by "The Misfit" were, events can summon our nation to take a second look at our values and lives. Tragedy and trash are only a click of a remote on our TV screens, and the world community often becomes the disposal bin of the waste product of the American media. Michael Amalodoss, commenting on how religion can address world conflict, argued that religion must challenge the practices and values that undergird social and economic structures and can foment injustice (*America,* 12/10/2001). He argued that every crisis, even the crisis of 9/11, is an opportunity, and concluded, "In short we need a conversion." What a strange combination of voices calls out to us: "The Misfit"; Jesus, who often does not fit in with people's expectation; and a learned Indian theologian who has often sent ripples of concern through the hierarchy. What does this conversion involve? Stay tuned for the journey through Matthew's Gospel!

PRAYING WITH SCRIPTURE

- Centuries before "The Misfit," St. Ignatius urged retreatants facing a significant life choice to ask what they would do if they were at the point of death. Pray over Jesus' summons to change of heart in similar fashion.

- The disciples hear the summons of Jesus while engaged in their ordinary daily work. Think how God's reign affects your daily life.

- Pray over those values in our culture that most need the healing grace of God.

Fourth Sunday in Ordinary Time

Readings: Zeph 2:3; 3:12-13; Ps 146:6-7, 8-9, 9-10; 1 Cor 1:26-31;
Matt 5:1-12a

"Consider your own calling, brothers and sisters"
(1 Cor 1:26).

THE MARKS OF THE TRUE CHURCH

The first of Matthew's five great discourses begins with an elegant and poetic set of blessings on those specially favored by God. The first four in Greek all begin with the letter "p" and speak of passive sufferers, the poor, the mourners, the gentle but strong (meek), and those starving and thirsting for justice. The second set praises those actively engaged in responding to God, people of integrity (clean of heart), the merciful (a major theme of Matthew), peacemakers, and not simply those who hunger and thirst for justice but who are persecuted in the quest. Both sets significantly end with a concern for justice.

The rhythmic structure, with two parallel panes of four Beatitudes each, is crowned by a ninth one, which switches from the third person, "Blessed are the poor," etc., to a dramatic direct address to the disciples: "Blessed are *you* when they insult *you,* and persecute *you* and utter every kind of evil against *you* falsely because of me" (5:11). This is most likely the evangelist's own formulation on the cost of discipleship, that is, persecution, which is being experienced by members of his community.

These dispositions praised by Jesus are open to misinterpretation. Matthew's addition of "in spirit" to a more original blessing on the poor (Luke 6:20) does not spiritualize poverty but emphasizes relying on God within the spirit, as opposed to depending on visible means of support such as wealth and the power it brings. The mourners are those who, like the psalmist of the Old Testament, lament the sufferings of God's people and complain about rampant injustice (see Pss 10; 22). Christian "meekness" is not a divinely sanctioned theology of Casper

Milquetoast, since Moses is described as the "meekest" of men. It is that strength that comes from nonviolent commitment.

In describing those attitudes and actions that bring God's blessing, I have used "justice" rather than "righteousness." The latter suggests personal piety and represents a religious patois that limits the impact of the Beatitudes. Imagine, for example, a "Righteousness Department" or a "Minister of Righteousness." Justice, instead, evokes the Old Testament motif of individuals and a community who are in proper relationship to God and neighbor. Proper relationships are a response to God's gift manifest in the liberation from Egypt and in the Sinai covenant. The Beatitudes take up again the great prophetic concern for justice and also anticipate the final words of Jesus, where the "just" are again blessed because they responded to the sufferings of their neighbors (Matt 25:31-45).

Another problem in interpreting the Beatitudes is a radical eschatological reading. The first and last Beatitudes promise the kingdom to the poor and those persecuted for justice, and the others speak of a future reward that parallels the attitudes of those blessed: the nonviolent meek will inherit the land, and the merciful will receive mercy. The future dimension is clear, but it is not necessarily an otherworldly future. For Matthew, the arrival of Jesus and his proclamation of God's kingdom create the conditions by which the world can be changed. The promise to the poor in spirit and those persecuted for justice that the kingdom of heaven is "yours" might better be translated as "on your side" or "for you."

The gospel today, last Sunday, and this coming Sunday lead us quietly into a Lenten journey of conversion and renewal. The dispositions and actions praised today by Jesus provide an alternate vision to contemporary, destructive attitudes and trends. Paul realized this when he said that God chose the foolish and weak of this world to shame the wise and the strong. Are Jesus' praises and Paul's declarations really too much for a contemporary Church to believe? Thankfully Lent comes every year.

PRAYING WITH SCRIPTURE

- Pray in gratitude for those who have guided you along the way of the Beatitudes.

- In prayer compose a series of beatitudes that should characterize Christians today.

- Pray for those Christians throughout the world who are insulted and persecuted because they live the Beatitudes.

Fifth Sunday in Ordinary Time
and Ash Wednesday

Readings: Isa 58:7-10; Ps 112:4-5, 6-7, 8-9; 1 Cor 2:1-5; Matt 5:13-16

> **"Light shall rise for you in the darkness**
> **and the gloom shall become for you like midday"**
> **(Isa 58:10).**

BEACONS OF HOPE

Lent is about to dawn and today's readings are a wake-up call. Even on a bleak February day the readings are suffused with images of light. Twice the prophet of Second Isaiah (first reading) tells the people that their light shall break forth like the dawn or rise in the darkness. It is not the light of victories in war or of resplendent worship, but giving your bread to the hungry, sheltering the homeless, and removing from your midst that malicious speech that can destroy a community.

The responsorial psalm heralds the person who is gracious, merciful, and just and gives to the poor. Such a one is a light in the darkness, and Jesus tells his disciples that they are the salt of the earth and the light of the world.

Images of light span the Bible. After the wind swept over the formless void, the first words spoken by God in the Bible are "Let there be light," and God saw "how good the light was" (Gen 1:3). The book of Revelation ends when God will give light to his servants forever (Rev 22:5). In a modern city, where technology can turn night into day, the contrast between light and darkness loses it force. In Jesus' time, darkness came suddenly, enveloping the whole land. Only from the light on a lampstand would the faces of others become visible. Light was a beacon to guide a travel-weary pilgrim; its faint glimmer signaled the beginning of a new day.

The disciples are pronounced salt of the earth. In the ancient world salt was used to flavor food, as a preservative, and often in sacrifice (Lev 2:13; Ezek 43:24). Though technically salt (sodium chloride) can never totally lose its flavor, it can be come adulterated and weakened. Jesus' image is simultaneously challenging and frightful. Disciples are like salt, necessary for life, and the call, once heard and given, can never be revoked, just as salt can never totally lose its flavor. But if the disciples abuse the call and grace of God, they are "no longer good for anything, but to be thrown out."

This section follows the Beatitudes, which describe the kinds of values a disciple should aspire to and precedes the contrast statements that describe the higher form of justice evoked by Jesus: renunciation of anger; marital integrity; honesty in speech; breaking the cycle of violence; forgiving enemies. At the Second Vatican Council the bishops, echoing Isaiah and this gospel, entitled their reflection on the Church as "light for the nations" *(Lumen Gentium)*. The United States bishops used these images in their 1994 statement *Communities of Salt and Light: Reflections on the Social Mission of the Parish,* which summoned people publicly to embody their faith by furthering the social ministry of the Church. Followers of Christ today are challenged to live those values expressed in the Sermon on the Mount, and so become salt of the earth and beacons of hope for others and perhaps signal the dawn of a new day. Lent provides a time to reflect on this mission.

Ash Wednesday

Readings: Joel 2:12-18; Ps 51:3-4, 5-6, 12-13, 14, 17; 2 Cor 5:20–6:2; Matt 6:1-6, 16-18

> **"Now is the acceptable time! Now is the day of salvation" (2 Cor 6:2).**

ID CARDS FOR THE PILGRIM CHURCH

As a newly ordained priest I was working with a military chaplain at a base in Germany. As we prepared for Ash Wednesday, he told me not to bless or distribute the ashes after the homily (the usual place), but to wait until the end of Mass. In his experience great numbers would come to church simply for the ashes and leave once they were smudged. His wisdom proved true as puzzled people huddled in the aisles throughout the Canon. Ashes on the forehead have become the once-a-year public signature for most Catholics.

And yet ordinary people symbolize a profound truth through this gesture. When confronting the crises of life, they realize that the Church offers signs of hope as we all realize that "we are dust and to dust we shall return." In an important work, *The Denial of Death*, the psychiatrist Ernest Becker noted that by not entering into the mystery of death, people waste their lives on palliatives. A man in his nineties, bent over with arthritis, walks slowly down the aisle, and a lively five-year-old little girl skips out of church, both carrying their credentials as ambassadors of reconciliation, a smudge that is a sign of the mystery of death and a promise of victory over it.

Lent is not simply forty days of repentance or change of heart in preparation for Easter, but the beginning of a pilgrimage that extends eighty days until Pentecost. The readings summon us to a return to a God who is "slow to anger and rich in mercy" (see Pss 86:15; 103:8), who gives back the joy of salvation and sustains a willing spirit "(Ps 51), and who knows how our hearts can turn quietly to him. Paul summons Christians to be ambassadors of reconciliation, because "God made him to be sin who did not know sin, so that we might become the righteousness of God in him" (2 Cor 5:21). Paul says that as we are reconciled to God, we enter an acceptable time, a day of salvation. This is the ultimate reason why people should stay (willingly, I would hope) for the whole Eucharistic liturgy. The signed foreheads signal a journey of renewal through death to all that wrenches us from love of God and neighbor, to the joy of victory over death at Easter, and hope for continuing life in the Spirit, when the dust of death shall be no more.

PRAYING WITH SCRIPTURE

- Read the Sermon on the Mount (Matthew 5–7), thinking of those parts that summon you to be a light to the world.

- Pray often the opening prayer of Ash Wednesday: "May this season of repentance brings us the blessing of your forgiveness."

- Ask God to transform you into ambassadors bearing a message of reconciliation.

First Sunday of Lent

Readings: Gen 2:7-9; 3:1-7; Ps 51:3-4, 5-6, 12-13, 17; Rom 5:19;
Matt 4:1-12

"For just as through the disobedience of the one man
the many were made sinners,
so, through the obedience of the one, the many will be
made righteous" (Rom 5:19).

Power Made Perfect in Weakness

Lent developed backward from a celebration of the Paschal Triduum, when the catechumens were baptized. After the conversion of the empire in the fourth century A.D., with the rise of infant baptism, the Good Friday and Easter Vigil fast was gradually extended to a forty-day fast, so the season was celebrated as an occasion of conversion for the whole Church. The renewal of the liturgy after the Second Vatican Council combines both of these emphases, but the readings for this cycle retain some of the most ancient readings for Lent.

The three great Johannine stories of coming to faith on the third, fourth, and fifth Sundays (John 4; John 9; John 11), with their rich symbolism of water and spirit, light and faith, death and life, provided an ideal baptismal catechesis. The Old Testament readings recount great events of saving history, especially those that prefigure the Gospel accounts. The first two Sundays in each cycle recount the testing of Jesus and his transfiguration, which are narrative forms of the famous hymn in Philippians 2:6-11: Jesus emptied himself, taking on the form of a slave, even to a slave's death, but was exalted by God so that every tongue might confess him as Lord. Since this hymn was most likely used very early at Christian baptism, it offered not only a theology of the Christ-event but a pattern to be imitated by Christians.

The traditional title "temptation" of Jesus is misleading, since today we interpret this term as enticement to sin. The Greek is better translated "testing" and reflects the Old Testament theme of the testing of righteous people (e.g., Job), the Servant of Isaiah 53 and the suffering just person, who, though tested by God, remains faithful and is called a child of God (Wis 2:12-20; 5:1-23; see Heb 2:18: "because he himself [Jesus] was tested through what he suffered, he is able to help those who are being tested.") Trial or testing also enables good people who undergo undeserved suffering to see in Jesus one who is compassionate and has suffered with them.

In contrast to Mark's simple statement that Jesus was tested forty days in the wilderness by Satan, Matthew and Luke have dramatic descriptions, derived from an earlier source, but revealing their distinctive theologies, expressed primarily in the order of the tests by Satan. In Matthew the final test, when Satan offers "all the kingdoms of the world," takes place on a mountain, as does Jesus' first great sermon (Matthew 5–7). On a mountain also is his final commission to the disciples to spread the gospel to all the world—when, ironically, those very kingdoms offered by Satan will now be claimed by the gospel.

Though Jesus' testing calls to mind the testing of Israel by God during the forty years in the wilderness (all but one of the Old Testament quotations are from Deuteronomy), they also evoke the original falling away of humanity in Adam. Satan introduces the first two tests with the phrase "If you are the Son of God . . .," which evokes the image of Adam created as a child of God. What the devil proposes to Adam and Eve is that they will be immortal and will be "like gods." Although human yet created in the image of God, they want to transcend humanity and usurp the power of the Creator. Jesus is then tested to show that he is Son by startling demonstrations of divine power: changing stones into bread and commanding the angels.

Jesus, whom Paul will call the last Adam, reverses the sin of Adam. Though called from birth "God with us," as the Gospel unfolds Jesus will not manifest his equality with God by demonstrations of self-serving power but will be called "a glutton and a drunkard, a friend of tax collectors and sinners" (Matt 11:19), as the servant who will not break the bruised reed (12:20), and as one who draws to himself those who labor and are burdened, not by overweening power, but by being meek and humble of heart (11:29). By accepting the fullness of humanity, Jesus is truly Son of God.

This Lent would be a good time to reflect on the massive horrors that have resulted over the last century from the quest for unlimited power, that originating sin which drives toward control over nature and other people. Christians should cringe every time they hear the refrain that we are "the most powerful (or better, power-filled) nation on earth." Throughout the world brutal dictators destroy the resources and spirits of their nations, and our ordinary lives often become miniature arenas of larger power struggles. Sadly, the quest for justice can be corrupted simply into a struggle for control. In our contemporary Church, polarization over liturgical minutiae often represents nothing more than a desire to lord it over others.

Jesus resisted this primal temptation toward misuse of power, while emptying himself so that we could experience true power: liberation from the fear of death through his passion and cross; confidence that even when we are of little faith, we can hear his words, "Take courage, it is I; do not be afraid" (Matt 14:27); openness to see his presence, not in the "kingdoms of the world in their magnificence," but in the least of his brothers and sisters (Matt 25:31-46).

PRAYING WITH SCRIPTURE

- In moments of trial or testing pray with Jesus, who was also subject to many trials.

- Pray often Psalm 51 (today's responsorial psalm) as a classic prayer for conversion and renewal of spirit through God's mercy.

- Pray over how issues of power and dominance can distort God's image in your life.

Second Sunday of Lent

Readings: Gen 12:1-4a; Ps 33:4-5, 18-19, 20, 22; 2 Tim 1:8b-10;
Matt 17:1-9

> **"This is my beloved Son,**
> **with whom I am well pleased;**
> **listen to him" (Matt 17:5).**

A VOICE FROM THE MOUNTAINTOP

As a diptych to the temptation of Jesus, the transfiguration is always proclaimed on the Second Sunday of Lent. The title masks its deeper meaning, since the earliest English use of "transfiguration" is for the feast, and it rarely appears in "secular" discourse. A better translation of the Greek would be the "transformation" of Jesus, which evokes the words of the hymn from Philippians that Jesus "took on the form of a slave, coming in human likeness" (Phil 2:7). The verb is found in only two other places: in Romans 12:2 ("Do not conform yourself to this age but be *transformed* by the renewal of your mind") and in a passage from 2 Corinthians 3:18, which shaped the theology of Irenaeus of Lyons and of Eastern patristic thought ("All of us, gazing with unveiled face on the glory of the Lord, are being *transformed* into the same image from glory to glory, as from the Lord who is the Spirit."). The manifestation of Jesus' glory is also a promise of the transformation of his followers.

The transfiguration comes at the beginning of Jesus' journey to Jerusalem after he has just proclaimed that it will terminate in a horrible death by crucifixion. Here a voice from heaven pronounces, "This is my beloved Son, with whom I am well pleased," echoing that same proclamation at Jesus' baptism (Matt 3:17). Jesus is the beloved Son not only when he announces God's mercy and love in the Sermon on the Mount and enacts God's victory over evil through his healing ministry but also when he enters into the mystery of suffering. In preaching on this feast, Karl Rahner reflected on what the event meant for Jesus himself: "This then is the meaning of the transfiguration for Jesus himself: in the dark night of hopelessness the light of God shines, a human heart finds in God the power which turns a dying into victory and into redemption of the world" (*The Great Church Year*, p. 342).

At the beginning of Lent the feast is also about the journey of Jesus' followers. Shortly before the ascent to the mountain, Simon Peter confesses Jesus as "Messiah, Son of the living God," and Jesus promises Peter that he will be the rock on which his Church will be built and that God's power will safeguard his mission. Yet when Jesus talks about his coming death, Peter takes him aside and says, "God, forbid Lord! No such thing shall ever happen to you." But afterward, gazing upon the glory of Jesus, flanked by Moses and Elijah, Peter wants to build three dwellings and rest there—no more talk of crucifixion. Peter's request is answered by a voice from a cloud-enshrouded mountaintop, proclaiming Jesus, as at his baptism, as God's beloved Son and charging Peter to "listen to him." Peter's "peak experience" is not an assurance of divine consolation, but a mandate to follow that very path of suffering discipleship, which he earlier resisted but which will be his ultimate destiny.

I have been writing these reflections on the anniversary of the birth of Martin Luther King, Jr. Thinking about the mountaintop, I read again his last speech, given the night before he died (April 4, 1968), a day that has seared my memory like the other horrors since that moment when as a little boy I first heard the words "day of infamy," unaware of how many such days lay ahead. Martin Luther King spoke with still unparalleled eloquence of the need for justice through nonviolence for the African American people, and especially for the exploited sanitation workers of Memphis. He spoke of the hopes of his people, not only for "long white robes over yonder" but for "suits and dresses and shoes to wear down here." At the end of the speech he said that he had been "to the mountaintop," and prophetically, "I've seen the promised land. I may not get there with you," but even so, "mine eyes have seen the glory of the coming of the Lord." Now thirty-seven years after his death, our nation must again "listen to him" and heed his message to follow the nonviolent quest for racial and social justice. His life, like that of Jesus, ended in a brutal and violent death. During this Lent, when violence and injustice are so much part of the air we breathe, we are challenged again to listen to him and to Him.

PRAYING WITH SCRIPTURE

• Repeat often the opening prayer of the liturgy: "Enlighten us with your word, that we may find the way to your glory."

- Recall "mountaintop" experiences of your life and remember how they strengthened you for the journey ahead.

- During this Lent pray especially for that peace that flows from justice and expresses itself in forgiveness (Pope John Paul II).

Third Sunday of Lent

Readings: Exod 17:3-7; Ps 95:1-2, 6-7, 8-9; Rom 5:1-2, 5-8;
John 4:5-42

"For Christ, while we were still helpless,
died at the appointed time for the ungodly" (Rom 5:6).

HIGH NOON!

The three great Johannine stories of coming to faith on the third, fourth, and fifth Sundays of Lent (John 4; John 9; John 11) date from the earliest celebration of Lent, since their dramatic character and rich symbolism of water and spirit, light and faith, death and life, provided an ideal baptismal catechesis.

The meeting between Jesus and the woman of Samaria is rich in Johannine symbolism and unfolds with many levels of meaning. Jesus rests at "Jacob's well," a site most sacred to both Jews and Samaritans, since it was named after Isaac's son Jacob, later called "Israel." While a woman coming to draw water at noontime is not surprising, the request of Jesus, a lone male addressing a woman in public, is shocking. The scene also recalls Old Testament meetings between future spouses at wells, for example, Jacob met Rebekah at the well of Haran, and Moses and Zipporah met at a well in Midian. The literary context of this meeting, as Sandra Schneiders notes, is nuptial, stretching from Cana (John 2:1-11) to Cana (John 4:46; see *Written That You Might Believe*). Jesus is "wooing" the Samaritan woman to true worship and to a mission of spreading the word.

After the initial surprise, the narrative focuses on the conversation between Jesus and the woman, using the familiar Johannine technique of misunderstanding to convey deeper truth. Jesus asks for a drink, and the woman responds with great surprise that he would even speak, no less request a drink, given the hostility between Jews and Samaritans. Jesus does not answer her objection but rather says that if she really knew the gift of God and Jesus' identity, she would be thirsting for living water. "Living water" has a profound double entendre, for it means fresh flowing water, not well water, and also that water which will give life. This emerges from the further misunderstanding of the woman and culminates in Jesus' statement that those who drink his water will never thirst and that this water will be a spring "welling up to eternal life." The woman asks for such water "so that I may not be thirsty or have to keep coming here." Again, the technique of misunderstanding, for she is really asking for something much more profound.

Jesus then asks the woman to bring her husband. When she replies that she has none, he says seemingly harshly that she is correct, since she has had five and is not really married to the present one. Bottles of ink and now printer cartridges have been expended on this interchange, ranging from earlier views that the woman was simply an adulteress to more recent opinions that the five husbands refer to the supposedly five foreign "masters" who imposed their religion on the Samaritans (2 Kgs 17:13-34).

Whatever the solution, the dialogue serves to evoke the woman's first confession of faith, "you are a prophet," and leads to a discussion of the locus of true worship, Jerusalem or Mount Gerizim. As with the living water, Jesus transcends the discussion by saying that the hour is coming when people "will worship the Father in Spirit and truth; and indeed the Father seeks such people to worship him." Now, in the person of Jesus, God becomes the suitor, wooing the woman to true faith, embodied in the woman's realization that the Messiah who will tell us everything is coming.

After an interlude of a discussion between Jesus and the disciples, the narrative returns to the woman, who has changed from a seeker to a missionary who told what Jesus had done, so that many Samaritans believed in him "because of the word of the woman who testified." Many then come to Jesus because of her testimony and believe, not because of the word of the woman alone, but because they meet Jesus, hear his word, and know that he is Savior of the world.

This narrative overflows with different meanings. On one level it is a paradigmatic story of a woman's coming to faith and becoming a missionary who brings others to Jesus, leaving to the Church a mandate to recognize the gifts and ministries of women. Coming to faith today involves immersion in the living water of baptism and rising up to bring others to Christ. It is also a narrative of God wooing the outsider, or as Paul will say, "the ungodly" (Rom 5:6). The Samaritans, who were considered godless, end up confessing Jesus as the Savior of "the world," not simply of his own people. The narrative also foreshadows that other noontime of Jesus on the cross (John 19:14), when he will again cry out "I thirst" (John 19:28), and a woman, his mother, will be given care of that disciple whom Jesus loved, himself a symbol of those who have heard the word of Jesus and have come to stay with him.

PRAYING WITH SCRIPTURE

- Pray over your own baptismal call to be a witness to Christ.

- Pray that religious hatred may be overcome so that people can worship in spirit and truth.

- In grateful prayer recall how women today witness to the new life in Christ and bring others to this gift.

Fourth Sunday of Lent

Readings: 1 Sam 16:1b, 6-7, 10-13a; Ps 23:1-3a, 3b, 5, 6;
Eph 5:8-14; John 9:1-41

"But now you are light in the Lord.
Live as children of light" (Eph 5:8).

SEEING WITH THE INNER EYE

The feast of Tabernacles (Sukkoth) was one of the great celebrations of the Jewish liturgical calendar. It was celebrated as an autumn harvest festival, when people built little booths or tents, which recalled their dwellings during their wilderness wanderings and their arrival into the land flowing with milk and honey. The days and nights were filled with singing and dancing and ceremonies in which priests carried water from the Pool of Siloam to pour in the Temple (perhaps as sacrifices for the coming rainy season). It was also a feast of lights as four great menorahs were set up in the Temple, so that "there was not a courtyard in Jerusalem that did not reflect the light of the House of Water Drawing " (Mishnah).

Jesus arrives to celebrate this feast earlier in the Gospel (7:2) and remains there through the feast of the Dedication (Hanukkah) in John 10:21. He engages in long debates over issues of his identity and relation to the Mosaic Law. Today's gospel is a narrative commentary on Jesus' earlier claims that he is the life-giving water (7:35-38) and the light of the world (8:12; see also 9:5). He appears only briefly at the beginning and end of the narrative, while the healing of the blind beggar is told very concisely so that "that the works of God might be made visible through him." The real drama in the story flows from the interaction between the blind man and his accusers *while Jesus is absent.*

After washing in the Pool of Siloam (interpreted as "one sent," that is, Jesus himself), the man returns "seeing" and is greeted by neighbors, who can't really believe that he was the one born blind. Ironically using one of Jesus' favorite self-designations, he replies "I am he." Asked how this happened, the man simply repeats what "the man Jesus" told him to do. Hauled next before the Pharisees, who are concerned about the sabbath healing, he again repeats what Jesus did, which precipitates a dispute among the Pharisees as to whether Jesus is "from God" (a theme that permeates John 7–10). When asked his view, the man says, "He is a prophet."

The Jewish leaders then summon the man's parents, who don't want to have anything to do with explaining the healing, since "he is of age; he can speak for himself." Summoned again before the leaders, the man is immediately confronted with the charge that Jesus is a sinner. The beggar's courage increases as he becomes a witness not only to what Jesus did but to who Jesus is, and taunts his accusers, asking if they want to become Jesus' disciples. Ultimately then he recalls the earlier question and says, "If this man were not from God, he would not be able to do anything." In anger they say he was born in utter sin and expel him from the synagogue.

Abandoned by his neighbors, rejected by his parents, and expelled from the synagogue, the man is "found" by Jesus, who asks, "Do you believe in the Son of Man?" When he asks who the Son of Man is, Jesus says, "You have seen him," a wordplay on sight suggesting that the real vision given to the man is that of faith. Then the man replies, "I do believe, Lord." The narrative concludes with the enigmatic statement of Jesus: "I came into this world for judgment, so that those who do not see might see, and those who do see might become blind." Ultimately the narrative is not simply about a contrast between people who are blind and those who see, but between those who know they are blind and those who claim to see.

This story provides a rich fare for Lenten reflection. Used as one of the Scrutinies (examinations of baptismal candidates), the motif of washing leading to sight anticipates baptism at the Easter Vigil. The blind man's brash fidelity during Jesus' absence offers John's persecuted community a model of courageous witness. Through opposition and persecution the blind man moves from a confession of "the man Jesus," to "prophet," to "worshiper of God," and finally to a confession of Jesus as the Son of Man.

Christians today who have been "enlightened" through baptism are commissioned to confess and witness to their faith when Jesus seems absent from their lives. Imitating the journey of the man toward greater insight about Jesus, Christians progress to an inner enlightenment, so that they can ultimately confess the crucified one as the Son of Man, who, when lifted up, will draw all things to himself. Lest the Jewish leaders be too harshly blamed, Christians today must ask about their own blindness. Recent Church statements have rejected the use of violence in the name of God, condemned racism, and preached tolerance for other religions. Yet history is replete with Church-sanctioned violence, racial prejudice, and religious intolerance. What blindness will future generations call us to account for? How can the healing power of Jesus lead us to true vision?

PRAYING WITH SCRIPTURE

- Pray with the opening prayer of the Mass: "May our faith, hope, and charity turn hatred to love, conflict to peace, death to eternal life."

- Scrutinize areas of contemporary blindness and ask God for true light.

- Pray over ways you might bring a healing touch to visually impaired people.

Fifth Sunday of Lent

Readings: Ezek 37:12-14; Ps 130:1-2, 3-4, 5-6, 7-8; Rom 8:8-11; John 11:1-45

> **"O my people! I will put my spirit in you that you may live" (Ezek 37:13-14).**

THE GIFT OF LIFE AT DEATH'S DOOR

Death has been too much our companion in recent years, not only from the disaster of September 11 but also from suicide bombings in Israel and Iraq, and the ever-mounting toll of people of all ages dying of AIDS. Death walks with Jesus in today's gospel as he moves in measured pace toward his own suffering and death. The raising of Lazarus is the final and greatest sign of Jesus, a symbolic narrative of his victory over death at the cost of his own life.

Three elements shape the theology and the dramatic tension: the message to Jesus from Martha and Mary, "Master, the one you love is ill"; Jesus' response that the illness is not to death, but for the glory of God that the Son of God may be glorified through it; and the editorial comment "Now Jesus loved Martha and her sister and Lazarus." Despite his love, Jesus remains two days before setting out for Judea. No other text in the New Testament speaks so often of Jesus' love—and of his subsequent grief.

Though Jesus never speaks *with* Lazarus, the conversations with Martha and Mary offer the most profound theology. They are models for Johannine Christians of their own journey to a profound faith. Martha meets Jesus and greets him with simple faith in his power as a miracle-worker: "Lord, if you had been here, my brother would not have died," yet with a deep trust that God will grant Jesus' request. As so often in this Gospel, Jesus simply transcends the question and says, "Your brother will rise." Again, the familiar Johannine technique of misunderstanding arises as Martha expresses faith in the common Jewish belief in the general resurrection of the dead "on the last day."

Jesus' reaction, which stands at the very center of the whole narrative, is to pronounce those words that bring such consolation at funeral services: "I am the resurrection and the life; whoever believes in me, even if he dies, will live, and everyone who lives and believes in me will never die" (John 11:25-26). Jesus says to Martha, "Do you believe this?" Somewhat strangely, Martha's answer has no direct connection with resurrection. She confesses Jesus in language stunningly similar to Peter's confession in Matthew 16:16-18: "You are the Christ, the Son of God." In this manner the evangelist tells us that to experience Jesus as the true life that conquers death, one must first accept that he is God's anointed Son.

The story then shifts to the meeting of Mary and Jesus, poignant and powerful. Mary was home weeping, but rose to greet Jesus with other Jewish mourners. Falling down, she worships him and speaks the very same words of simple faith as Martha had. Unlike with Martha, Jesus does not respond immediately, but the evangelist tells us that he was "perturbed and deeply troubled," strong language expressing Jesus' anger at death's power and sorrow over its ravages. Jesus goes to the tomb, and in one of the most extraordinary incidents in the New Testament at the door of death, which has become the barrier between himself and one he loves, "Jesus wept" tears of loss over a loved one.

Arriving at the tomb, Jesus is again perturbed and orders the stone to be removed. Martha reappears and her words are another instance of John's technique of misunderstanding. In the colorful words of the King James Version, she says, "Lord, it has been four days and he stinketh," which, like the realism of Jesus' anger and grief, enhances the realism and horror of death. After praying to his Father, Jesus cries in a loud voice, "Lazarus come out," and "the dead man" emerges totally wrapped in the burial shrouds. Lazarus will die again, but Jesus, whose burial cloths are left in the tomb, is the giver of life who will never die.

This gospel provides a wealth of reflection as Holy Week approaches. Jesus offers "eternal life," which begins with faith *now* and lasts forever. "Eternal life" in John is not primarily unending life but "authentic life," or life in its fullness. Both Martha and Mary are models of people coming to a deep faith even in the face of doubt. No section of John captures as well the great paradox of John that Jesus is from above, the "Word [who was] with God and [who] was God" (John 1:1), yet truly became flesh.

Like centuries of his devoted followers, Jesus weeps in the face of death. As Sandra Schneiders says eloquently in her study of John 11, "Eternal life conquers death without abolishing it," and "we are asked not to weep, but only not to despair, for the one in whom we believe is our resurrection, because he is our life" *(Written That You Might Believe)*. Since the raising of Lazarus leads the Jewish leaders to agree that Jesus must be killed, Jesus here is a model of greater love who lays down a life for a friend, which will be played out between now and Easter.

Praying with Scripture

- Pray that like Martha and Mary you may hold to faith in God in the face of the death of loved ones.
- Visualize Jesus weeping at the tomb of one he loved, and stand with him in moments of deepest grief.
- Pray frequently the words of Jesus: "I am the resurrection and life; whoever believes in me, even if he [or she] dies, will live."

Palm Sunday of the Lord's Passion

Readings: Isa 50:4-7; Ps 22:8-9, 17-18, 19-20, 23-24; Phil 2:6-11;
Matt 26:14–27:66 (longer form) or 27:11-54 (shorter form);
Matt 21:1-11 at the procession with palms

"He emptied himself, taking the form of a slave"
(Phil 2:7).

A MEMORY: JOYFUL AND SUBVERSIVE!

What an extraordinary scene etched on the wall of a second-century Roman building like some graffito at a big-city underpass! A line-drawn figure gazes at a crucified donkey, with the rough inscription "Alexamenos adores his God." Before crosses adorned our churches and glimmered on jewelry counters, the cross was a symbol of disgrace and mockery, and yet drew people to silent adoration. The paradox of the cross is captured on Palm Sunday. Jesus enters Jerusalem with royal acclamation, not astride a horse but "meek and riding on an ass," a symbol of peace, not war. At the end of this week, a placard on the gibbet of the cross proclaims him king in the truest sense, one who rules by self-giving, one who wins by losing.

The density and drama of the readings for Palm Sunday present a challenge to preaching and reflection. Recognizing this, recent liturgical directives allow the use of only one reading before the gospel or even reading the Passion alone due to pastoral needs of particular congregations. The Passion accounts, which bracket Palm Sunday and Good Friday and culminate in the resurrection proclamation, are invitations to engagement and contemplation. Unlike many liturgies that have become overly wordy and passive, Holy Week engages the whole community in bodily movement. People solemnly process on Palm Sunday; have their feet washed on Holy Thursday, move silently and reverently to kiss the cross on Good Friday, and walk with candles at the Easter Vigil. A people on the move through history are caught up flesh and spirit in the unfolding drama of the cross and resurrection.

I witnessed a striking image of the power of these symbols at St. Claire's parish in Santa Clara, California. Every Good Friday the parish celebrates the way of the cross by moving to different stations throughout the neighborhood. The huge crucifix is lifted from the front wall of the church and the Portuguese marching band, beating a somber rhythm, leads the procession. The parish is ethnically diverse, and each group carries the cross for a number of stations: Portuguese, Chinese, Latinos, Anglos, and Vietnamese. Young and old are united as one mingles with a grandmother in traditional dress holding the hand of a granddaughter in jeans and an Oakland Raiders jacket; little children run back and forth, often evoking frowns from prayerful parents. The event is a powerful symbol that whatever our differences and heritage, we carry Christ's cross together.

Matthew's Passion has distinctive vignettes of Jesus' path to Calvary. Matthew introduces major sections with the title "Jesus," which readers know from the angel's command (1:27) means "he will save his people from their sins." Jesus in his first great discourse praises those who are persecuted for the sake of justice (5:10), and is condemned after Pilate's wife warns him not to have anything to do with this "righteous man" (27:19). Even Judas repents when he realizes he has betrayed "innocent blood" (27:4). Matthew's Gospel and Passion narrative are permeated by the theology of Jesus as the suffering just person who will "proclaim justice to the Gentiles" (12:18) at the cost of his own life. Matthew alone recounts the earthquake at Jesus' death, when tombs are opened and many of the saints are raised, a vivid symbol that death is conquered at the very moment of its apparent victory (27:52-53).

A special pathos accompanies us this Holy Week as we recall the indiscriminate, inclusive horror inflicted on people by terrorism and war in recent years and the lasting grief of so many. With Christ on the cross this year are those who gave their lives trying to save others, as well as those whose lives were simply snatched away. Matthew's Passion also reminds us of those people who seek justice by speaking out on behalf of the poor and the marginal or who unmask the hidden structures of evil, often at the cost of their lives.

In an essay entitled "The Rose Garden," Jon Sobrino, S.J., describes a garden that was carefully tended by Obdulio, husband of Elba, who was killed along with her daughter Celina and six Jesuits in El Salvador in November 1989. He speaks of the need to keep alive the joyful and subversive memory of the cross and says that Christians must unite "against that part of the cross which is sin, and in support of that part of the cross which is joy." This memory is subversive, since it summons us to view the world with the clear eyes of victims, not through the prism of the powerful, which can be rotated to show things in an ever-changing and more agreeable light. From Alexamenos to the pilgrim people of San Jose, and with those who come to the rose garden with tears and love, the journey of Holy Week remains our greatest mystery—and our greatest hope.

PRAYING WITH SCRIPTURE

- Pray often the opening Mass prayer: "Help us to bear witness to you by following his example of suffering, and make us worthy to share his resurrection."

- Imaginatively construct your own way of the cross and ask Christ to walk with you.

- Pray over how the mystery of the cross and resurrection unites people today.

Easter Sunday: The Resurrection of the Lord

*Readings: Acts 10:34a, 37-43; Ps 118:1-2, 16-17, 22-23; Col 3:1-4
or 1 Cor 5:6b-8; Matt 28:1-9*

> **"For you have died and your life is hidden with Christ
> in God" (Col 3:3).**

FROM DEATH'S DOOR TO THE PATH OF LIFE

*Dic nobis Maria, quid vidisti in via; sepulchrum Christi viventis et gloriam
vidi resurgentis*—"Yes, tell us again, Mary, what did you see on your
journey?" "I saw the tomb of Christ who still lives and the glory of the
risen one." The core of Easter faith resounds through these words from
the cadenced Easter sequence. Mary Magdalene, whose love brought
her to the cross and who watched as Jesus was wrapped for burial, was
last seen in the Gospel sitting at the tomb. After the Sabbath she and the
other Mary came again to the tomb, the abode of the dead, and were
the first to see it emptied of its power and to experience the presence of
the risen one.

Each Easter morning Gospel has its own distinctive beauty. The
women arrive at dawn, symbolically the dawning of a new day in human
history, and Matthew alone recounts an earthquake, which often sym-
bolizes the punishment of God's enemies as a prelude to the resurrection of the dead (see Matt 27:4; Rev 11:13-19). Only Matthew records
that the angel, who in Jewish tradition guides the just to heaven, rolls
the stone away and sits on it, another visual symbol of the victory over
death.

The most distinctive elements of Matthew's version then emerge. In
fear the guards become lifeless, the first of four indications of "fear" in
the narrative. The angel then tells the women, "Do not fear," and announces that Jesus has been raised from the dead. They are then commissioned as the first heralds of the resurrection, and, unlike Mark's
Gospel, where they say nothing, they leave quickly "with fear" and joy,
only to be met by Jesus. Falling in worship and grasping his feet, a clear

indication that the risen Jesus is not simply a spirit, they hear from Jesus the same words uttered by the angel: "Do not fear, go and tell my brothers to go to Galilee and there they will see me."

We live today in a culture of fear, nurtured by a media that conducts an up-to-the-minute feeding frenzy on every horror in our world. As I write these lines, death seems far more victorious than life: another day of slaughter in Israel, with more children sacrificed on the altar of violence and hatred; gruesome details about the brutal murder of a child in San Diego; headlines about a mother who killed her children in Illinois; multiple killings of Hindus on an Indian train, with expected reprisals— all in a single day. Will our night of sitting at death's door be followed by the dawn of life's new day?

Today's gospel speaks of two kinds of fear. The fear of the guards makes them like the corpse they were supposed to watch over, and yet they too rush to deliver a message—to the chief priests. They do not end up in faith and joy; rather they perpetuate a false report. There is a fear that can paralyze people and blind them to the light of truth. The fear of the women at the words of the angel take us back to the very beginning of the Gospel, where an angel says to Joseph, "Do not fear," and commands him to take Mary as his wife. From her womb will come forth Jesus, who will save his people, just as the crucified one has come forth from the tomb. The fear of the women is then transformed to fear with joy, that mysterious sense that God has touched their lives in a unique but mysterious way. As they grasp the risen Jesus, they hear again the words "Do not fear." Only joy remains.

The Easter proclamation is not simply a happy ending to a tragic story. It captures the unending rhythm of confrontation with suffering and death transformed by life. The women were seeking not Jesus the teacher, but "the crucified one," and heard that death could not contain him. These women, faithful followers and heralds of the resurrection, have many brothers and sisters today who nurture a culture of love and joy in the face of death. Fundamentally, such people believe that death is not the meaningless end of life, but the door to the fullness of life with the risen Christ, who in his transformed humanity remains one of us, wounded and transformed. They are those Christians whose fear does not lead to a distortion of the truth but to joyful proclamation, and who enact a gospel of joy and life in their daily lives. The women ran from the door of death to proclaim the word of life. Shall we follow?

PRAYING WITH SCRIPTURE

• Pray for the newly baptized that they may becomes joyous heralds of the risen Christ.

- Pray often over the words of the angel, "Do not be afraid . . . you are seeking Jesus the crucified. He is not here, for he has been raised, just as he said."

- Pray in gratitude for those people who touch your life with the joy of the resurrection.

Second Sunday of Easter

Readings: Acts 2:42-47; Ps 118:2-4, 13-15, 22-24; 1 Pet 1:3-9; John 20:19-31

"Although you have not seen him, you love him"
(1 Pet 1:8).

DIRECTIONS TO THE NEAREST CHURCH

The period from Easter to Pentecost celebrates the presence of the risen Christ in the Church. The gift of the Spirit to the fearful disciples and the appearance to "doubting Thomas" complete the Easter octave, when early Christians doffed the white robes of baptism and entered the period of instruction into the deeper mysteries of their faith. Until Pentecost, the first reading is always from the Acts of the Apostles, which might be better called "the Acts of the Holy Spirit," since every important event in the early Church is stimulated by the Spirit. The second reading is always from 1 Peter. Prayer and reflection during this period could do no better than meditative reading of Acts and 1 Peter, which is an eloquent exhortation for Christians to realize their dignity as "a chosen race, a royal priesthood, a holy nation, a people of his own" (1 Pet 2:9).

People frequently ask, "What is the Church?" and today's readings provide foundational images for God's own people. Three motifs characterize the appearance to Thomas: the greeting of peace, a gift of the risen Christ that casts out fear; the presence of the Holy Spirit manifest in the power to forgive and restrain sin; and the need for a faith that grows even without the tangible presence of Christ. Every Christian who envies the Easter experience of Jesus' first followers can pray daily Jesus' words to Thomas: "Blessed are those who have not seen and have believed."

The reading from Acts (along with its parallel in 4:32-37) provides "marks" of the early Church that should define the Church throughout the ages. It is a community (the etymological meaning of the Greek *ekklēsia*) called forth by the Spirit and characterized by *koinōnia*, "communion," less accurately "communal life" (NAB), devotion to the apostolic teaching *(didachē)*, to the breaking of the bread, and to prayer. This picture is often dismissed as a utopian view of Christian origins or as an example of early Christian "communism," which necessarily collapsed under the weight of historical accretion. The emphasis on communion and "holding all things in common" is a way of expressing the Hellenistic idea of friendship. A friend was a person with whom one held all things in common, considered to be the highest form of love. The stress on selling property and meeting the needs of others countered those major barriers to true friendship in antiquity, which were disparity of class and wealth.

Since Vatican II there has been unparalleled reflection on the nature of the Church. Increasingly the magisterium and theologians of different stripes have stressed a model of *communio*. Though all share a foundational vision of communion with Christ through the Holy Spirit, its implications are open to different interpretations. Curial theologians seem to understand it primarily as "vertical," that is, communion under the explicit direction of Rome, so that local and regional institutions are reduced primarily to implementing Vatican directives.

Today's readings image a horizontal communion, a communion of friends gathered in fidelity to the apostolic teaching and in breaking of bread and care for those in need. Though obviously a bit simplistic for complex modern society, the New Testament models indicate that communion is to form the institution, and not be subordinated to it. Though early in the sex abuse scandal a leading U.S. cardinal affirmed that he was not a CEO, the public face of the Church and its centralized authority often mirror a bureaucracy. Church spokespersons often communicate in an ecclesiastical patois similar to "Enronese."

While this may be true of the "vertical" Church or the Church "from above," the Church "alongside of" throughout the land provides great images of hope. Thousands of people conclude their journey through the RCIA, united as a community of friends. Parishes continually seek creative ways to bridge the gap between the prosperous and the needy. Scripture and the "teaching of the apostles" are presented often through well-informed homilies and by thousands of lay religious education teachers. In its social ministry the Church confronts those evils that corrode our society. Young parents are handing on the faith in new, creative ways. Whatever dark shadows have fallen over the priesthood in recent months, dedicated men, young and middle-aged, prepare to be good servants of God's people, sympathetic to those excluded from priestly ministry. All this is ultimately due to power "from above," the gift of the Holy Spirit given at baptism. There is ample reason during this Paschaltide to hear Jesus' message of peace and to offer praise to

God in sharing our eucharistic banquets with "joy-filled and sincere hearts, praising God" (Acts 2:46-47, *au. trans.*).

PRAYING WITH SCRIPTURE

- Both 1 Peter and Acts stress Christian joy. Reflect on that true joy that fills your life.

- Pray in gratitude for the newly baptized or those now in full communion who offer images of hope today.

- Pray over ways that your local parish or community may be a gathering of friends.

Third Sunday of Easter

Readings: Acts 2:14, 22-33; Ps 16:1-2, 5, 7-8, 9-10, 11; 1 Pet 1:17-21;
Luke 24:13-35

"Were not our hearts burning within us
while he spoke to us on the way?" (Luke 24:32).

GOING MY WAY

The journey is one of the oldest biblical symbols. Abraham hears the command to become a "wandering" Aramean; Israel makes a journey through the wilderness, where they are covenanted with the living God. Luke groups Jesus' most distinctive teaching under the journey to Jerusalem (Luke 9:51–19:28), while Acts is a series of journeys in an ever-widening circle outward from Jerusalem. Many find God as pilgrims to Lourdes, Knock, or Compostela and metaphorically as they embark on new life courses. The gospel is a narrative parable of post-resurrection faith for Luke's pilgrim community and for the Church through history.

Two people are leaving Jerusalem, in animated conversation about their shattered hopes. One is named Cleopas and the other, though unnamed, is identified by significant scholars as "Mary the wife of Clopas," whom John places at the cross (John 19:25), perhaps a veiled reference to the early Christian practice of missionary couples (for example, Priscilla and Aquila). An unknown stranger joins them and asks, "What are you discussing?" Words spill out, constituting the longest speech in the Gospels by someone other than Jesus, culminating with the poignant words "We were hoping that he was the one to redeem Israel." They knew of the crucifixion and reports of the resurrection, but this did not fit into their deepest hopes. They knew and loved Jesus the Messiah, but for them he was a messianic prophet, like Moses, mighty in deed and word before God and all the people. Their hopes for Jesus were for a strong liberator who would free the land from Roman domination and punish sinners.

Such a hope appears in the *Psalms of Solomon,* most likely from the first century B.C.: "Wisely, righteously he [the hoped-for Son of David] shall thrust out sinners from (the) inheritance; / He shall destroy the pride of the sinner as a potter's vessel. / With a rod of iron he shall break in pieces all their substance, / He shall destroy the godless nations with the word of his mouth; (*Ps Sol* 17:23-24). Such a hope is reflected in the Canticle of Zechariah, who praises God for sending a mighty savior to liberate the people from their enemies (Luke 1:69-71). The two disciples on the way to Emmaus recall the story of the warrior God who delivered the people out of Egypt and destroyed the Egyptians. This was the kind of Messiah they hoped for.

But a different story is now told. Luke recounts Jesus' reply to their shattered hopes: "'Was it not necessary *(edei)* that the Christ should suffer these things and enter into glory?' Then beginning with Moses and all the prophets, he interpreted to them what referred to him in all the scriptures" (Luke 24:26-28). This combination of messianic suffering as a sign of God's will revealed in Scripture appears at other crucial places in Luke-Acts (Acts 3:18; 17:3; 26:22). The problem long puzzling to exegetes is that there are no clear places in the Jewish Scriptures where the Messiah, that is, the anointed and hoped-for Davidic king, would suffer and die. Commentaries generally note this and perhaps call attention to the motif of the Suffering Servant, but then move forward to other parts of this rich narrative.

This passage is most significant in understanding Luke's theology of forgiveness in the post-resurrection Church. Luke summons his readers in effect to *tell a new story of God.* The old story that was kept alive by people in the hope for a royal, conquering Messiah, the earthly counterpart of the divine warrior, has been supplanted by a new story of the suffering and dying Messiah, the earthly counterpart of a God who, in the words of the theologian James Alison, "wins by losing."

The story that Jesus told them was totally new and just did not fit in. They awaited a Messiah who would conquer enemies; Jesus was a Messiah who was killed by enemies and spoke final words, not of conquest, but of prayer to his Father: "Forgive them for they do not know what they do." The people on the journey felt that Jesus was a prophet who would unmask sinners, yet Jesus is a prophet who embraces a weeping woman as her tears wash over his feet and tells her that her sins are forgiven because she has loved much. A Messiah who conquers sin by compassionate love and subdues enemies by reconciliation and forgiveness—this is the new Easter story that Jesus tells them.

Today's gospel is really a parable about the continuing journey of the post-Easter Church. The people's true understanding of the resurrection comes as Jesus breaks open the word of Scripture and breaks bread with them—an icon of eucharistic liturgies through the centuries. But through the centuries the Church, like the man and woman on the first

Easter eve, too often wants to live the old story. This old story is one of power and violence, which prefers a prophetic Jesus, mighty in word and deed, who vanquishes enemies, rather than a Jesus who brings peace and forgiveness to enemies by instructing his disciples to put away their swords. The new story of Jesus is of one who preaches and practices forgiveness of sin, in a Church that often seems more interested in the prevention of sin. And yet Jesus tells us that *it was necessary that the Messiah should suffer and die.* Why necessary? Only by this great act of love and forgiveness, of being the victim of violence rather than its perpetrator, did Jesus tell the new story of a God who wins by losing.

This parable of a post-Easter journey unfolds with more levels of meaning. The Emmaus pilgrims' true understanding of the resurrection comes as Jesus breaks open the word of Scripture and breaks bread with them, an icon of the eucharistic liturgy. A critical turning point comes when Jesus feigns to leave and they offer him hospitality. Hospitality to the stranger who might bear the presence of Christ was one of the earliest and most enduring Christian practices. Their journey of shattered hope becomes one of vision transformed, an allegory perhaps of many Christians' pilgrimages throughout the centuries. The approach of evening and the waning day suggest that Christ may enter and transform the lives of his disappointed followers when shadows fall over their flagging spirits or in the eventide of life. At his birth the Messiah brought consolation and joy to older people (Anna and Simeon). Age is no barrier to the power of God's presence and word to set hearts aflame and to transform lives.

Vatican II described the Church as the "pilgrim people of God." This has waned in recent teaching; pilgrimages tend to be messy and often unstructured. Now the Church moves more like a tightly orchestrated procession with clearly assigned places. Many ordinary people continue their pilgrimage silently, with the thought "We were hoping," Today's gospel and Luke's whole theology of the Spirit, which will unfold in Acts, is a chronicle of the way God can walk with us in surprising, often unknown ways, reversing our path from fear and disappointment to make of us bearers of the power of the Risen One.

PRAYING WITH SCRIPTURE

- Imaginatively place yourself with the disciples on the way to Emmaus. Hear their questions and listen again to the words of Jesus.

- Remember when God has transformed shattered hopes into new opportunities.

- Pray that Christ may enter the life of a loved one who journeys in sadness or doubt.

Fourth Sunday of Easter

Readings: Acts 2:14a, 36-41; Ps 23:1-3a, 3b-4, 5, 6; 1 Pet 2:20b-25;
John 10:1-10

> **"I came so that they might have life**
> **and have it more abundantly" (John 10:10).**

THE WAY OF THE SHEPHERD

On this Good Shepherd Sunday all cycles of liturgical readings use excerpts from John 10. Segmenting this chapter presents major problems, for the distinctive Johannine theology emerges only from John 10:1-18. Today's reading is an appetizer before the main course. Jesus tells an initial parable (10:1-6) warning against thieves and robbers who do not enter the sheepfold through the gate, in contrast to the shepherd who enters the gate, calls his own sheep by name, and walks ahead of them, for they recognize his voice. There follows a double application of the parable in which Jesus is both the gate and the shepherd.

The shepherd imagery is deeply rooted in biblical thought. God is the ultimate shepherd of the people, providing guidance, sustenance, and protection (Ps 23); kings and other leaders were to be shepherds of their people. Israel's hopes for the end time included a messianic figure who, like David the shepherd king, would gather in the people. One of the interesting ways in which the evangelist John refashions the traditions about Jesus found in the other Gospels is by making Jesus himself the subject of parabolic images. In Matthew (18:10-14) and Luke (15:3-7) Jesus tells of a shepherd who seeks a lost sheep; in John, Jesus is the "good" shepherd who will lay down his life for the lost. In the Synoptics Jesus tells parables about vineyards where God is the owner (Mark 12:1-2, and parallels; Matt 20:28-32), while in John, Jesus himself is the vine and the disciples are the branches (John 15:1-11) The parable giver of the Synoptic Gospels becomes the parable of God in John.

The designation "good" for Jesus contrasts with the frequent designation of unfaithful leaders in Israel as bad shepherds who abuse and neglect the flock (see especially Ezek 34). Though not proclaimed in this Sunday gospel, the distinctive Johannine addition to the shepherd imagery of the Bible is a shepherd who will lay down his life for his flock, which includes sheep not of "this fold," so there will be "one flock" and "one shepherd" (John 10:16), a verse that motivated Pope John XXIII when he envisioned the Second Vatican Council.

The paschal season calls us to reflect on the distinctive Johannine contribution to "pastoral" ministry. John's Gospel shows little interest in structured roles and offices and lacks any appointment of twelve apostles; the beloved disciple, not Peter, is given pride of place. A Johannine disciple is not chosen to govern or even proclaim the gospel but to be a faithful witness who brings people to Jesus. The "pastoring" is done by Jesus, who knows and listens to the sheep. He is also their way, truth, and life, and true disciples form a community of friends known by their self-emptying love.

Since January 2002 we have been inundated by a deluge of public reports on "bad shepherds," with resulting mudslides of explanation, recriminations, and justified pain and anger. Such sad events may be a wake-up call to reflect on John's vision of a community characterized by a love that brings people to Christ and a truth that will make them free. Catholic theology is often a combination of Johannine Christology (with a tilt to the "divine" side of truly divine and truly human) and Matthean ecclesiology (with a tilt to Matthew 16:13-20). A new Church may emerge with a Johannine ecclesiology and a Matthean Christology—"Come to me all you who labor and are burdened and I will give you rest" (11:28).

PRAYING WITH SCRIPTURE

- Pray with Psalm 23, pausing over verse 4: "Even though I walk in the dark valley, I fear no evil; for you are at my side."

- Jesus, the Good Shepherd, "knows" his sheep; speak familiarly to him as to a friend.

- Repeat the words of the closing prayer: "Attune our minds to the sound of his voice, lead our steps in the path he has chosen."

Fifth Sunday of Easter

Readings: Acts 6:1-7; Ps 33:1-2, 4-5, 18-19; 1 Pet 2:4-9; John 14:1-12

**"You are a chosen race, a royal priesthood,
a holy nation, a people of his own" (1 Pet 2:9).**

CHRISTIANS, RECOGNIZE YOUR DIGNITY!

As the Easter cycle moves to Ascension and Pentecost, the readings foreshadow the ongoing life of the Church. The Acts of the Apostles describes an early conflict in the community and the choice of seven men filled with the Spirit. One is Stephen, who immediately afterward is put to death, which causes the Church to spread outward from Jerusalem. Peter exhorts his community of "chosen sojourners" who suffer persecution by recalling their dignity as followers of Christ, and Jesus begins his final instructions to his disciples with the simple exclamation "Do not let your hearts be troubled. You have faith in God; have faith also in me."

Despite the idyllic picture of the Church early in Acts as a community of friends who shared all in common, so that there was no needy person among them (Acts 2:42-47; 4:32-35), with growth comes dissension over the daily food distribution between the Hebrew- and Greek-speaking members. The Twelve ask the whole community to pick seven persons filled with wisdom and the Spirit to supervise the charitable work so that they may devote themselves "to prayer and to the ministry of the word."

Curious elements surface in this account. Though called the selection of "deacons," the term is not used, and the phrase "to serve at table" can mean "to supervise the distribution." Also, none of the seven are mentioned again apart from Stephen, who is martyred because of his mighty works and powerful preaching (not inner community service) and Philip, later called "the Evangelist," whose four daughters are prophets (Acts 26:7-10). The important element in this passage is the presence of the Spirit in the Church, which leads the Twelve to consult and follow the decision of the whole community as new needs and ministries emerge.

Jesus' Last Supper discourse in John 13–17, which contains some of the most memorable of Jesus' sayings, prepares the disciples for his future departure and the coming of the Paraclete (or Advocate), who will instruct them profoundly about the nature of Jesus and the kind of community they are to become. The chapters are difficult to excerpt for a particular Sunday, since they are both repetitive (for instance, John 16 repeats much of John 14) and yet carefully structured.

Today's gospel follows Jesus' statement that he is going where the disciples cannot follow until later. (Johannine irony permeates this passage, since Jesus is going to his crucifixion; the disciples will not follow but will do so later). After telling his disciples that they know the way, in another instance of misunderstanding leading to deeper truth, Philip naively asks how the can know the way if they do not know where he is going. Jesus responds "I am the way and the truth and the life," which can be understood as "the way," which is both truth (that is, the unveiling of God) and life, themes that have permeated the Gospel. These themes will culminate when Pilate stands before Jesus and asks, "What is truth?" The reader knows the answer: Jesus is the truth who ultimately has power over Pilate.

The next section shifts to Jesus' relation to the Father (one of mutual knowledge and indwelling) and the need for faith and trust in him, concluding with the remarkable statement that "Whoever believes in me will do the works that I do, and will do greater ones than these, because I am going to the Father." These words anticipate the coming of the Advocate (14:25-31), who is the continuing presence of Jesus in the Church. The "greater works" have long puzzled commentators but seem to be the disciples' works of faith and love to be done through the centuries in imitation of Jesus and by the power of the Spirit.

Both John and 1 Peter offer a lofty vision and challenge for the Church today. Peter tells his beleaguered community that they are "a chosen race, a royal priesthood, a people of his own" who will proclaim the praise of God. Beginning in January 2002 and continuing sporadically, recent years have been "the worst of times," a season of discontent, as the daily papers chronicled ever more cases of sexual abuse by priests and the sad history of fumbling attempts of Church leaders to deal with this, along with the heartrending reactions of victims and "God's own people." Earlier in his letter Peter described the faith of his community as "more precious than gold that perishes, though it is tested by fire." The recent crisis is a summons to reflect on the deepest ground of our faith. Lives of faith and hope offered to God are the sacrifice that makes of us all "a royal priesthood." The thousands of people who entered the Church this past Easter and the millions who live and hand on the faith do so, not because a particular bishop, pastor, or teacher is virtuous, but because they find Christ, who leads us along the path to truth and life.

Praying with Scripture

- Think prayerfully over your life as a "priestly ministry" that offers praise to God.

- Pray especially for those "new Catholics" as they approach the mystery of Pentecost.

- Pray in gratitude for those "greater works" that have accompanied your way to God.

Sixth Sunday of Easter

Readings: Acts 8:5-8, 14-17; Ps 66:1-3, 4-5, 6-7, 16, 20; 1 Pet 3:15-18; John 14:15-21

"I will not leave you orphans; I will come to you" (John 14:18).

WAITING FOR A GOOD LAWYER!

Whether a John Grisham novel, a prime-time TV series, or a host of films from "To Kill a Mockingbird" to "Philadelphia," courtroom dramas provide enduring fascination. Especially frequent are plots pitting a little-known lawyer defending a victimized client against powerful adversaries. This appeal is as early as the biblical stories of Susanna and the elders in Daniel 13 and the woman judged for adultery in John 8. John's Gospel has been described as a long trial narrative in which the powers of the world are arrayed against Jesus, culminating in his carefully orchestrated appearance before Pilate. On the evening before he departs this life Jesus warns his disciples that a fate similar to his awaits them. The world that hated him will hate them (15:18); they will be rejected and "the hour is coming when everyone who kills you will think he is offering worship to God" (16:2). They will be hauled before the court of the world to be witnesses to the teaching of Jesus.

Yet Jesus will not leave them as orphans but will provide a defense attorney for his followers when they are brought to trial. Older translations following the Greek called this helper a "Paraclete," literally "one called alongside of," an "advocate" (a legal metaphor). This Advocate is also the "Spirit of truth," (14:17) and the "Holy Spirit," whom "the Father will send in my name," who will teach you all things and bring to your remembrance all that I have taught you and who will be both advocate and defense witness (15:26). As Jesus has come into the world, so too the Advocate, who is teacher and guide; the Advocate will, like Jesus, bear witness in a situation of hate. The Advocate (Paraclete) is then the enduring presence in the Church of the departed Jesus, who prolongs his life and teaching through history.

Karl Barth is reported to have said that as Christology was the focus of the twentieth century, the role of the Spirit will be the focus of the present century, a prediction verified by renewed interest in both theology and Church life. Too often in the past the Spirit has been invoked as either the guarantor of fixed teaching or even a behind-the-scenes "fixer" who will remedy human error ("Well, I hope the Holy Spirit knows what he or she is doing!"). Jesus promises the Advocate to those who keep his commandments, but in John these are not primarily moral precepts but the call to radical faith and radical love. The Holy Spirit is present when the kind and quality of life embodied in the Word-made-flesh is visible to the world. Such is the best legal advice as we prepare for our trial.

PRAYING WITH SCRIPTURE

- In times of trial think of the Spirit of Jesus as your Counselor and Advocate.

- Repeat the phrase from today's opening prayer: "Help us to celebrate our joy in the resurrection of the Lord and to express in our lives the love we celebrate.

- During this season of "confirmations" pray for those young people who will receive the gift of the Spirit.

The Ascension of the Lord

When the Ascension of the Lord is celebrated on the following Sunday, the second reading and gospel from the Seventh Sunday of Easter may be read on the Sixth Sunday of Easter.

Readings: Acts 1:1-11; Ps 47:2-3, 6-7, 8-9; Eph 1:17-23; Matt 28:16-20

> **"Go . . . teaching them to observe all that I have commanded you" (Matt 28:20).**

TIME TO MOVE OUT!

In one of the annual preached retreats I was subjected to as a young Jesuit, the director presented a vivid picture of the ascension (long before the age of shuttle launchings). As Jesus rose heavenward, he saw Jerusalem, Nazareth, Galilee, Asia Minor, Greece, and finally Rome. This is just what the feast is *not* about, since what are celebrated are Jesus' exaltation and the end of his earthly existence as a prelude to the gift of the Spirit. This exaltation embodies one of the oldest christological confessions, Philippians 2:6-11, where one who was in the form of God emptied himself, becoming obedient to death on a cross, only to be exalted and given a name at which every knee would bend and every tongue would confess that Jesus Christ is Lord. This is also the pattern of the theology of Luke and John.

Yet my retreat master, perhaps too taken up himself with the journey through the heavens, had a great insight. Before his departure Jesus commissions his disciples as "witnesses in Jerusalem, throughout Judea and Samaria and to the ends of the earth" (Acts 1:8). Jesus would "see" these places as the Spirit-directed Church moves outward from Jerusalem. Such is the "exocentric" theology of Acts. In a rhythm of persecution and repeated impulses of the Spirit, the Church in Acts moves from Jerusalem to Rome, where the imprisoned Paul, "with complete assurance, and without hindrance proclaimed the kingdom of God and taught them about the Lord Jesus Christ" (28:31).

One of the major phenomena of the past fifty years has been the spread and growth of the Church far beyond the confines of Luke's vision. Jesus' commission in Matthew to travel to the ends of the earth making disciples of all nations seems a reality. Recently I noticed that the greatest number of Jesuits in the world now live and work in India, while other parts of Asia and Africa represent areas of greatest growth. As in Acts, persecution and often murder are the cost of faithful witness to the gospel, especially as people speak out on behalf of the poor and marginal (another strong theme of Luke-Acts). In the United States and in the West generally, the Church is preoccupied with internal problems, often of its own making.

The feast of the Ascension tells us that the Church must be a community in mission guided by God's Spirit and confident of God's protection even amid suffering and death. But mission is not something we see by gazing beyond the horizons of our own land, but a summons, especially to a younger generation of Catholics, to move to uncharted territory under the guidance of God's Spirit, with confidence in Jesus' final words in Matthew: "I am with you always, until the end of the age."

PRAYING WITH SCRIPTURE

- Apply the prayer of Ephesians to your own community: "May the God of our Lord Jesus Christ, the Father of glory, give us a Spirit of wisdom and revelation resulting in knowledge of him."

- Pray in gratitude for the riches that people from the ends of the earth bring to our Church.

- Pray in hope that as Christ was raised to glory through suffering, so too will his followers.

Seventh Sunday of Easter

Readings: Acts 1:12-24; Ps 27:1, 4, 7-8; 1 Pet 4:13-16; John 17:1-11

"Hear, O Lord, the sound of my call" (Ps 27:7).

THE WHISPER OF TRUTH

Since most dioceses have transferred the Ascension to this Sunday, preaching on these readings will be relatively rare. Yet they contain rich resources for reflection as the Church awaits the reenactment of the gift of the Spirit at Pentecost. The Acts of the Apostles offers an illustration of the life of the early community as it awaits the power the Holy Spirit will bring. Since Luke is always anxious to portray the early community as faithful to its Jewish heritage, he noted at the end of the Gospel that they returned with great joy and worshiped in the Temple every day. Here he notes that the mount called Olivet was a Sabbath day's journey (following Jewish law), but he describes a different kind of prayer. The disciples return to the upper room, the site of Jesus' last meal, where Luke mentions eleven disciples and then explicitly notes the presence of "some women," and Mary the mother of Jesus and his brothers. The picture is iconic and idyllic as they devote themselves "with one accord to prayer."

Prayer is one of the major and most important themes of Luke-Acts. From the annunciation to Zechariah through the Ascension and Pentecost and then throughout Acts, major events in salvation history occur when people are at prayer. Both Zechariah and Mary offer canticles of praise; Anna and Simeon are models of prayerful fidelity as they await the Messiah; and prayer is the prelude to major events in the life of Jesus. In Acts "breakthrough" events occur in a context of prayer, for example, the selection of the "deacons" (6:1-6); the command to Peter to eat unclean food and thus welcome Gentiles into the community (10:9-17); and major events in the Pauline mission. Only Luke tells significant parables of prayer, such as the need for boldness in the face of opposition of the friend at midnight (11:5-8) and of courage in the face of injustice in the story of the poor widow who fights for her rights before an unjust judge (18:1-8), while the tax collector's prayer that as a sinner all he can do is ask for God's mercy wins favor (18:9-14). On Calvary the prayer of a murderer for remembrance by Jesus is answered by a promise of eternal life (23:42-43).

In no other area must Christianity always tap into its Jewish roots than in thinking about prayer. Before the psalms were called "the prayer of the Church," they echoed the praises, the sorrowful laments, and joyful hymns of the people of Israel. In our century no author has expressed both the beauty of prayer and its utter importance better than Abraham Joshua Heschel (1907–1972), a teacher, scholar, and prophet for all people. For Heschel, prayer is not a human quest for God, but is epitomized in the title of one of his major books, *God in Search of Man.* In one of his most profound comments, he describes prayer as "an invitation to let God intervene in our lives." In a comment meriting quoting in full, he goes on to say:

> Our approach to the holy is not an intrusion by an answer. Between the dawn of childhood and the door of death, man [today we would say men and women] encounters things and events out of which comes a whisper of truth, not much louder than stillness, but exhorting and persistent. Yet man listens to his favors and whims, rather than to the gentle petitions of God. The Lord of the Universe is suing for the favor of man (*I Asked for Wonder: A Spiritual Anthology,* ed. Samuel H. Dresner [New York: Crossroad, 1985]).

The gospel presents the first part of Jesus' final words to his disciples, often called "Jesus' High Priestly Prayer," because here, in language incomprehensible apart from his Jewish heritage, he prays that his Father glorify his Son, that he become a Father to his disciples and make them holy, and prays for those who through the word of the disciples may come to know his Father. Jesus' last testament is that his followers be brought into that kind of loving union with the Father that he shares.

Rediscovery of the importance of prayer has been one of the major achievements of Church life in recent decades. Newspaper articles and TV reports regularly comment on the crowding of monasteries and centers of prayer where lay people set aside "the favors and whims" of life to listen for "the gentle petitions of God." From the shattering events of September 11, 2001, through the horrible shame of sexual abuse, Catholics (and others) experienced their equivalent of Queen Elizabeth II's *annus horribilis* (1992 speech to parliament after her sons' marriage breakups and fire in Windsor Castle). Yet God remains in search of us, suing for our favor. Amid world problems and ecclesial scandals shine forth the words of Heschel: "Dark is the world for me for all its cities and stars. If not for the certainty that God listens to our cry, who could stand so much misery, so much callousness?" (*I Asked for Wonder*, 21).

PRAYING WITH SCRIPTURE

- As Ordinary Time approaches, think of how prayer can become an extraordinary part of ordinary life.

- Think of Sunday liturgy as gathering in prayer and hope with Jesus' mother, his disciples, and brothers and sisters.

- Listen for those "gentle petitions" that God is making in your life.

Pentecost Sunday

Readings: Acts 2:1-11; Ps 104:1, 24, 29-30, 31; 34; 1 Cor 12:3b-7, 12-13; John 20:19-23

**"Lord, send out your Spirit,
and renew the face of the earth" (Resp. Ps.).**

Born of the Holy Spirit

The annual celebration of the paschal mystery that began on Ash Wednesday culminates at Pentecost in a narrative that evokes major Old Testament themes. Acts recounts the overwhelming gift of the Spirit. Such a fresh outpouring of the Spirit was to accompany the messianic age. Also, by the first century Pentecost, which occurred fifty days after the Passover, memorialized the covenant at Sinai. Having celebrated the liberating Passover sacrifice of Jesus, the disciples are formed into a covenant community that is to continue the work of Christ throughout history. As we celebrate the traditional birth of the Church, the readings present the genetic code of the living Church.

Pentecost mandates that the Church be aware of its universal mission. At Babel, humans who tried to raise themselves to God were splintered by different languages (Gen 11:1-9); at Pentecost, when God's power descends, there is no longer a confusion of tongues, but wonder as people from the four corners of the earth hear the apostles in their own languages. One of the most fundamental human divisions is broken down. Through the Spirit further barriers are surmounted, especially in the "Pentecost of the Gentiles" (Acts 10), when cultural religious practices are transcended. In our time no miracle easily surmounts these divisions, but the legacy of Acts summons the Church to shape its life to different languages and cultures. Fundamental to this is translating the Bible and liturgical books into the vernacular in a manner adapted by the local culture so that all can "hear" in their own languages. Recent moves in the Church to either restore Latin or make translations uniform scarcely reflect the message of Acts.

The Pauline reading speaks of another kind of Spirit-given diversity in the Church. In 1 Corinthians, Paul writes to a community divided by problems that would encourage any pastor today to plan for early retirement. Initially there are factions gathered around particular leaders, followed by a host of strange sexual problems (a form of incest, visiting prostitutes); a theological food fight; marital problems; questions on women's' participation in public worship; and disputes over the celebration of the Lord's Supper—all less than a generation after the death of Jesus. Paul responds by recalling the significance of the Christ-event, for example, those who feel free to eat food offered to idols he writes, "Through your knowledge, the weak person is brought to destruction, the brother [or sister] for whom Christ died" (1 Cor 8:11).

Paul adapts his responses to specific problems, becoming "all things to all . . . for the sake of the Gospel" (1 Cor 9:22-23). His pastoral theology is epitomized in 1 Corinthians 12, where he celebrates different kinds of spiritual gifts but the "same Spirit," in that each individual is given the manifestation of the Spirit for the benefit of the whole body. Throughout the whole chapter, diversity and mutual interdependence are manifestations of the Spirit's presence and gifts to the Church. Claims to precedence and privilege destroy the unity and harm the whole body.

The Johannine "Pentecost" occurs on Easter eve, when Jesus appears to the frightened disciples with a twofold greeting of peace. These disciples who fled in fear at Jesus' arrest are now themselves forgiven and are commissioned to continue his mission from the Father. Though they had abandoned Jesus, he will not abandon them ("leave you orphans," John 14:18); though they failed Jesus, God's love will not fail them. Then, reminiscent of God's action at creation, Jesus breathes on them, saying, "Receive the Holy Spirit. Whose sins you forgive are forgiven them, and whose sins you retain are retained." "Retaining sin" should not be equated simply with a juridical act, since the Greek *(kratein)* can also mean "restrain" or "hold in check." Through the gift of the Spirit, who is also the Spirit of truth, the disciples are given power to forgive sin and unmask and control the power of evil.

The infant Church, born of the Holy Spirit and nurtured by its presence, has grown in wondrous and varied ways and finds new dwelling places: "Because the Holy Ghost over the bent / World broods with warm breast and with ah! bright wings" (Gerard Manley Hopkins, *God's Grandeur*).

Praying with Scripture

• Pray to the Spirit in the words of the Pentecost sequence: "Heal our wounds, our strength restore."

- Thank God for the different gifts and ministries that continually renew the Church

- Say often the prayer composed by Pope John XXIII before the Second Vatican Council: "Renew your wonders in this our day as by a new Pentecost."

The Most Holy Trinity

Readings: Exod 34:4b-6, 8-9; Dan 3:52, 53, 54, 55; 2 Cor 13:11-13;
John 3:16-18

> **"Live in peace, and the God of love and peace**
> **will be with you" (2 Cor 13:11).**

A Mystery Almost Too Good to Be True!

Though the most profound mystery of Christian faith, this feast presents a great challenge to all Christians, and especially on a Sunday morning in May. The traditional expression of the doctrine, three Persons in one God, is puzzling to contemporary people, for whom "persons" often means "people" (even though they realize that this is not really true of the Trinity). In my pre-ordination theology study four decades ago, the treatise on the Trinity was the Rubik's cube of theology, summarized in the old saw: four relations, three Persons, two processions, one God, and no proof—and, I would add, little seeming relevance to our spiritual lives.

The best place to find how the Trinity shapes our lives is the article "Trinitarian Spirituality" from the *Collegeville Dictionary of Spirituality*, edited by Michael Downey and the late Catherine L. LaCugna and published by the Liturgical Press, Collegeville, Minnesota. Some phrases capture its dynamism: "[T]he doctrine of the Trinity affirms that it belongs to God's very nature to be committed to humanity and its history, that God's covenant with us is irrevocable, that God's face is immutably turned toward us in love, that God's presence to us is utterly reliable and constant"; "[T]rinitarian spirituality is one of solidarity between and among persons. It is a way of living the gospel attentive to the requirements of justice, understood as rightly ordered relationships between and among persons."

Though not explicitly Trinitarian, the readings convey the fundamental mystery that the Triune God reaches out to people in love, seeking the deepest communion. The reading from Exodus follows the apostasy of the people in worshiping the golden calf. Moses again ascends the mountain to intercede, offering his own life for the people. This evokes yet another revelation of God (Lord = Yahweh) as "a merciful and gracious God, slow to anger and rich in kindness and fidelity," truly a God who knows the suffering and weakness of humanity and is constantly summoning them back to his love and mercy.

The selection from John contains one of the most-quoted New Testament texts, chiseled into churches and paraded as a bumper sticker, usually just "John 3:16" ("God so loved the world that he sent his only Son, so that everyone who believes in him might not perish but might have eternal life.") The God who heard the cries of his people in Egypt, witnessed their affliction, and came down to save them (Exod 3:7-10) now sends his Son, the Word-made-flesh (John 1:14) so that "the world," that is, everyone who believes in him, may be saved.

Though the first half of the gospel is constantly cited as an index of God's love, the last phrases (most often left out) raise questions today: "Whoever does not believe has already been condemned, because he has not believed in the name of the only Son of God." There are Christian groups today who believe that explicit belief and confession of Jesus as Savior are necessary for salvation, which leads at times to heroic missionary activity, as it once did for missionaries such as St. Francis Xavier. Contemporary Catholic theology wrestles with this issue by stressing the necessity of explicit faith juxtaposed with the statement of Vatican II that salvation is possible for "those who, through no fault of their own, do not know the Gospel of Christ or his Church, but who nevertheless seek God with a sincere heart, and, moved by grace, try in their actions to do his will as they know it through the dictates of their conscience" (*Dogmatic Constitution on the Church*, no.16).

The Gospel of John does not present a theology of non-Christian religions but is written both for fence-sitters like Nicodemus (3:1-15) and for John's persecuted community. He cautions about those who "preferred darkness to the light because their deeds were evil." For John, "judgment" is not something that happens at the end of history but takes place within history as people consciously choose evil over good and turn away from the covenant God of love, mercy, grace, and truth (see 1:16-17). The ultimate mystery is that the Trinitarian God who reaches out in love is the same God gives freedom to reject that love.

The solemnity of the Holy Trinity offers the foundation of Christian hope. We are loved not by a distant God but by one whose Son offered up the very life of God for our sake. The Church today lives in the gift of the Spirit from Father and Son, which forms us into sons and daughters of God (Gal 4:1-7). This Spirit, who touches all those who are created in the image and likeness of God and who bear the imprint of the last Adam, is capable of leading people who love the light into ever more profound unity and reconciliation.

PRAYING WITH SCRIPTURE

- Repeat prayerfully the words from Exodus: "The Lord, the Lord, a merciful and gracious God, slow to anger and rich in kindness and fidelity."

- Pray over how God's love has touched your world.

- Bring to God in prayer people you know who find it difficult to believe in God's love.

The Most Holy Body and Blood of Christ

Readings: Deut 8:2-3, 14b-16a; Ps 147:12-13, 14-15, 19-20;
1 Cor 10:16-17; John 6:51-58

> **"Because the loaf of bread is one,**
> **we, though many, are one body" (1 Cor 10:17).**

REMEMBERING THE PAST, PROCESSING TO THE FUTURE

Though today's feast almost seems like an appendix to the solemn liturgy of Holy Thursday and solemnizes what we believe in every liturgy, it provides a wonderful overture to the resumption of Ordinary Time. The feast originated in the visions of St. Juliana of Mount Cornillon (1193–1258) and was celebrated first as a local feast but was extended to the whole Church by Pope Urban IV in 1264. It was primarily a processional feast that quickly spread throughout Christendom. St. Thomas Aquinas composed the Divine Office for the feast. The Eucharist was carried throughout a town or village, and the processions grew into dramatic reenactments of the whole course of salvation history. The risen Christ, present in the Eucharist and in the Church, accompanied people throughout their ordinary lives, and in many parts of the world the feast is still celebrated with traditional rituals involving music and dance. The feast is a classic example of liturgy "from below," as each culture paints the festival in different hues.

In the first reading God is the leader and companion on the people's journey. Moses addresses a people about to enter the Promised Land and summons them to "remember" the saving deeds of God, reminding them that it was by God's power and love, not their own, that they had been released from slavery, while warning them of the perils that await if they abandon God's command. The possession of the land they will enter is contingent on their fidelity to the covenant.

The Pauline selection and the gospel speak more directly to the themes of the feast. In this section of 1 Corinthians Paul is involved with various disputes among his fractious community over eating food offered to idols and attendance at pagan banquets. Today's reading is a snippet in which he argues that all sacrifices, Christian (10:1-17), Jewish (10:18) and pagan (10:18), establish a form of communion *(koinōnia)* with the God to whom the sacrifice is offered. In sharing the cup of blessing and breaking bread, Christians celebrate communion with the body of Jesus broken on the cross and the blood poured out for us. This creates the deepest union among Christians, a union that is threatened by participation in pagan banquets. Most likely Paul here addresses people in the community with greater resources and social standing who will also distort the meaning of the Lord's Supper by shaming the "have nots" (1 Cor 11:17-26).

Motifs from the Exodus events permeate the gospel. Throughout John 6, Jesus contrasts the food that he will give to the manna given in the desert. Bread in this chapter has the double sense of wisdom from heaven as well as the bread of life, which is Jesus himself. The stark realism of the language "eat flesh" and "drink blood" emphasizes that the life of the Word-made-flesh and his death on the cross brings eternal life to the Christian. Eternal life is fullness of life with God in Jesus.

A number of fruitful themes emerge from this feast. The image of a procession of ordinary people following the enshrined Host, often carrying symbols of their trade or craft, recalls our procession through life and reminds us that the Eucharist is our food for the everyday journeys of life. These journeys mix the joy of resurrection with the sorrow over a death, the death of Jesus on the cross. The Eucharist we receive and enshrine is never simply a meal or an object of adoration, but a memorial of a life given for others and a summons to seek the kind of communion with God and others that Paul proclaims. Often in today's Church (well rooted in Corinth), the Eucharist is a source of division. Paul does not address this division by taking sides; later he will say that he and other Christians who know that idols are folly can eat food offered to them but should refrain from eating if it presents an obstacle to the weaker brother or sister (1 Cor 10:23–11:1). The important thing is union *in* Christ, not disputes *about* him.

Historically, the feast also reminds us of the importance of liturgy "from the people." In our century as in no other, the Church has taken root in many diverse cultures. Just as devotions and ritual emerged in the Middle Ages, which celebrated how God's love touched ordinary life, contemporary cultures will add to the rich tapestry of Catholic devotion. Pope Urban IV approved the feast and processions of Corpus Christ because they expressed the faith and devotion of the people. What wisdom does a thirteenth-century pope offer today?

PRAYING WITH SCRIPTURE

- Pray over the words of the opening prayer, which describes the Eucharist as "a solemn pledge of undivided love."

- Pray over how the Eucharist may become a greater sign of unity in your parish and daily life.

- Thank God for the wonderful unity amid cultural diversity that graces the Church's procession into a new millennium.

Tenth Sunday in Ordinary Time

*Readings: Hos 6:3-6; Ps 50:1, 8, 12-13, 14-15; Rom 4:18-25;
Matt 9:9-13*

"Abraham believed, hoping against hope" (Rom 4:18).

THE MANNER IS EXTRAORDINARY

The Lectionary returns to "Ordinary Time," under the guidance of Matthew. Until the Twenty-Fourth Sunday of the year, the second reading excerpts major sections of Romans, rather ironically, since some scholars hold that Matthew's Gospel was composed to counter certain Pauline attitudes in the Church. Matthew has always been the favorite Roman Catholic Gospel, while Romans has provided a canon within the canon for churches of the Reformation. The Lectionary provides a fine opportunity to preach on, pray over, and study these two documents and to be grateful for the growing reconciliation between divided members of the Christian family.

Serendipitously, today's readings, in their stress on mercy, faith, and love (see Matt 23:23), provide a wonderful introduction to the riches of Ordinary Time. Of all the prophets, Hosea may best express the merciful and loving compassion of God. In a context excoriating false repentance (Hos 5:15–7:2), the prophet quotes insincere attitudes and counters them with an oracle from God: "Your piety is like a morning cloud, like the dew that early passes away," while God desires "love . . . not sacrifice, and knowledge of God rather than holocausts" (6:6).

The gospel appropriately relates the call of Matthew and the complaint of the Pharisees that Jesus eats with tax collectors and sinners. Indiscriminate association with the marginal is one of the most solid traditions about the historical Jesus, so much so that before he was ever called "Lord" or "Messiah," his earthly description was "a glutton and drunkard, a friend of tax collectors and sinners" (Matt 11:19). As in Mark, Matthew defends his actions with a proverb about the sick, not the well, needing a physician but adds to his Markan source the quote from Hosea 6:6 on the primacy of love and mercy over false devotion (see also Matt 12:7).

The story of Abraham completes the triad of love and mercy. Throughout Romans 4, Abraham is a model of a faith that brings about a right relation to God, rather than human achievement. Powerfully stated by Paul: he "believed, hoping against hope." Though he and Sarah were past the age of bringing forth new life, he never forgot God's promise of an heir; he never "weakened in faith," nor did he ever doubt God's promise. This depth of faith that brings forth life from death enables a person to trust in Jesus, who was handed over and raised up "for us."

Today's brief readings offer challenges for the Church today. True religion involves a deep faith in the mercy of God, which issues forth in love. Hosea challenges false repentance, where "the most beautiful words cannot save an ugly heart" (Carroll Stuhlmueller, *Collegeville Bible Commentary*, 504), and images a God who seeks mercy and love. Jesus enacts God's mercy by associating with religious outcasts while challenging people's conception of who is the "insider" and who the "outsider." The faith of Abraham reminds us that before there was any Judaism or Christianity, God was active in history, and this same faith summons us to think of possibilities of reconciliation between the three great Abrahamic faiths: Judaism, Christianity, and Islam. Ordinary Time presents some extraordinary challenges.

PRAYING WITH SCRIPTURE

- Hosea says that God "will come to us like the rain, like the spring rain that waters the earth." Pray with this image on a rainy day.

- Pray over how the Church might embody God's mercy to outsiders today.

- Thinking of Abraham "hoping against hope," place your deepest hopes before God.

Eleventh Sunday in Ordinary Time

Readings: Exod 19:2-6a; Ps 100:1-2, 3, 5; Rom 5:6-11;
Matt 9:36–10:8

> **"You shall be to me a kingdom of priests,**
> **a holy nation" (Exod 19:6).**

AND PRESSING IS THE MISSION

While last Sunday's readings stress the gifts of God that guide Christian life, the readings today stress the need to reach out to others. The reading from Exodus introduces the whole sojourn of the wandering people at Sinai, where God announces that they are to remember God's saving deeds and to be faithful to the covenant. They are commissioned to be "a kingdom of priests, a holy nation" (19:6), which in the New Testament is applied to the whole Christian people (1 Pet 2:5, 9).

The gospel falls into three parts: the picture of Jesus as the compassionate shepherd; his choice and empowering of "twelve disciples"; and his commission to them to participate in his mission. Each element is important. "Compassion," in both Greek and Hebrew, is related to the word used for "womb" and suggests deep inner feeling where life unfolds. Jesus' compassion arises over the sheep who are literally harassed and lying on the ground. His actions (Matt 9:35) and attitude contrast with that of the bad shepherds (leaders) of Ezekiel 34:4, who "did not strengthen the weak nor heal the sick nor bind up the injured . . . [nor] bring back the strayed nor seek the lost [see Matt 18:10-14], but you lorded it over them harshly and brutally."

Out of compassion, Jesus then summons twelve disciples and commissions them with the same power that he possesses. The "Twelve" represent an institution that goes back to the historical Jesus and most likely reflect his self-understanding as one who will restore the twelve tribes of Israel (see Matt 19:28), especially since the names vary, while the number remains constant. As an *institution*, "the Twelve" does not continue in early Christianity, though their *mission* of imitating Christ through service to the suffering continues in the Church's pastoral (shepherding) ministry.

After calling the Twelve, Jesus sends them out as itinerant missionaries who are to continue his mission with reliance on God rather than human acceptance. Unlike Mark, in Matthew Jesus and the disciples are not to enter non-Jewish territory. In Matthew the mission to the nations, which was anticipated by the visit of the Magi, is the task of the post-resurrection Church, summoned then to make "disciples" of all peoples (Matt 28:16-20).

The outreach to all people emerges strongly in the reading from Romans, which is the very heart of Pauline theology. Last week Jesus stated that he did not come to call the just but sinners. Paul says that Christ died for the "ungodly" and for sinners who are reconciled to God by Christ's death and who are now saved by his life, that is, the enduring presence of Jesus of Nazareth as the risen one. The motif of imitation implicit in Matthew becomes explicit as Paul told the Galatians: "For all of you who were baptized into Christ have clothed yourselves with Christ" (3:27).

For preaching and reflection, we might think of the Church as a community always in mission, confronting with compassion those who suffer and are in thrall to evil. As Christ died for "the godless," the Church has a mission to those who have not experienced God's love. "Pastoral" ministry in the Church should reflect the compassion of Jesus, not the quest for power like Ezekiel's leaders.

Praying with Scripture

- St. Paul says that Christ died for "the ungodly." Pray in a special way for those who do not experience God's love.

- Reflect on how God's mercy, love, and gift of faith have sustained your life.

- Pray that God will continually send more laborers for his harvest.

Twelfth Sunday in Ordinary Time

Readings: Jer 20:10-13; Ps 69:8-10, 14, 17, 33-35; Rom 5:12-15; Matt 10:26-33

"Do not be afraid of those who kill the body but cannot kill the soul" (Matt 10:28).

A New Age of Martyrs

A decade ago I was privileged to be a delegate at the Thirty-Fourth General Congregation of the Society of Jesus meeting in Rome. The main work of the Congregation was the revision of the different laws that direct Jesuit life, as well as responding to questions raised throughout the Jesuit provinces about our life and mission today. Though people are aware today of the documents issued by the Congregation, some of my most vivid memories are of the people attending and of the liturgies. For the first time since the onset of the Cold War, Jesuits came in significant numbers from former Iron Curtain countries, along with an ever-increasing number of Asian and African Jesuits. Many of these brought not only wisdom but stories of a life of suffering for the gospel. Father Emil Krapka, for example, with whom I worked as a member of one of the commissions, had been an underground priest in Slovakia, with hands scarred by hard manual labor. Father Joseph Doan, the first Vietnamese representative to a General Congregation, had spent a number of years in prison.

One evening we had a liturgy of martyrs, recalling not only those of past Jesuit history but more those of the past half century. People from every part of the world processed in with banners listing those who had been killed, most often because of their dedication to the marginal and their opposition to injustice. Karl Rahner once remarked that in this century the tradition of martyrs who die as witnesses to the faith is now supplemented by witnesses for justice. I knew of those who had died in El Salvador and Zimbabwe, where I had visited freshly dug graves in the summer of 1978, but the extent and number simply overwhelmed me. The faith and courage of my dead Jesuit brothers both inspired and shamed me. Recently I read through Robert Royal's *Catholic Martyrs of the Twentieth Century* (New York: Crossroad, 2000) and realized that the Jesuit experience was but one patch in a multicolored mosaic of lives given for others throughout the world, including great numbers of women religious and lay women ranging from El Salvador to Sierra Leone.

These martyrs come to mind as I reflect on the readings for this Sunday. After castigating the leaders for not obeying God's word, Jeremiah is scourged and put in stocks by Pashhur, the head of the Temple police. Throughout his long career Jeremiah criticized the power elite for their neglect of the poor and for their reliance on foreign entanglements rather than on God. Later he was thrown into a cistern to die (Jer 38:1-13) and was released only through the intercession of the Ethiopian court official Ebed-melech. In later Jewish tradition Jeremiah was martyred in Egypt.

Matthew 10 is one of the Gospel's five great discourses. Commonly called the "Mission Discourse," Jesus instructs the disciples about the conditions and challenges of continuing his mission. Today's gospel is both sobering and consoling. The disciples will face lethal opposition but should not fear "those who kill the body, but cannot kill the soul" because they are under God's loving care and will have Jesus as their ultimate vindicator.

The Church today is a community of martyrs (witnesses) no less than when Christians were thrown to the lions. Today's lions are powerful figures and institutions that are unmasked by people who imitate the prophets and Jesus. Though most of us are not called literally to give our lives, the modern martyrs' love of "the least of Jesus' brothers and sisters" and their concern for truth and justice are mandates for all of us.

PRAYING WITH SCRIPTURE

- Pray in gratitude for those contemporary martyrs and their loved ones.

- Repeat often in prayer the words of Jesus to his disciples: "Fear not."

- Pray with the words of today's psalm: "In your great kindness answer me with your constant help" (Ps 69:14).

Thirteenth Sunday in Ordinary Time

*Readings: 2 Kgs 4:8-11, 14-16a; Ps 89:2-3, 16-17, 18-19; Rom 6:3-4,
8-11; Matt 10:37-42*

**"If, then, we have died with Christ,
we believe that we shall also live with him" (Rom 6:8).**

To Give and Not to Count the Cost

The gospel today continues last week's theme of "the cost of discipleship," with the added motif of hospitality to the prophet (first reading). Following Jesus is a commitment to companionship and mission
that can surpass the most precious things in life, relations with loved
ones, and bring about suffering and even loss of life. Generations of
Christians have struggled with the Lukan version of this saying, where
the would-be disciples are told they must "hate" parents and relatives
(Luke 14:26-27), which is not only contrary to the Ten Commandments
but shocking on the lips of Jesus. Matthew gives the proper interpretation of the term "hate" by writing that the one who loves family "more
than me" cannot be a true disciple. Family love is not abandoned but
enhanced. Matthew also alters the harshness of the tradition by adding
the sayings on hospitality, where everyone who gives one of the "little
ones" even a glass of water will be rewarded.

Today, when the average life span is twice that of the time of Jesus,
the love of Jesus, which transcends even natural affection, can be expressed in paradoxical ways. Often young people seeking their own
way in the world or responding to a particular call from God can enter
into conflict with parents. Later in life, care for parents and friends who
are aged and infirm can be a manifestation of care for the "little ones"
praised by Jesus. Such love can be a daily taking up of the cross and
losing one's life in care for those very people who literally gave life and
lived in service of their children.

These demands of Jesus would seem harsh and unrealistic were it
not for the insight Paul offers. Two weeks ago Paul proclaimed that "God

proves his love for us in that while we were still sinners Christ died for us" (Rom 5:8), and today he unfolds the implications of this gift: the Christian is one who through baptism has already lost his or her life by dying with Christ but now can walk in the newness of life. The daily cost of discipleship and the ultimate surrender of ourselves to God are not simply ethical demands, but an expression of gratitude for gifts received.

PRAYING WITH SCRIPTURE

- Paul tells the Romans that they must be dead to sin and live for God in Christ Jesus (Rom 6:11). Pray over what this means in your life.

- In moments when life seems most threatened, recall Jesus' words: "Whoever loses his [or her] life for my sake will find it."

- Think of times when, by receiving one of the "little ones," you have received Christ.

Fourteenth Sunday in Ordinary Time

Readings: Zech 9:9-10; Ps 145:1-2, 8-9, 10-11, 13-14; Rom 8:9, 11-13;
Matt 11:25-30

> **"Come to me all you who labor and burdened,**
> **and I will give you rest" (Matt 11:28).**

AFTER THE PARADE IS OVER!

Independence Day! From sea to shining sea: parades streaming down Main Street, band concerts of patriotic music, fireworks displays, cookouts—all celebrating the birth of a nation with paeans of praise for freedom, democracy, and military might. With the memory of 9/11/2001 and ongoing global conflict ever fresh, the celebrations will be bittersweet. How inappropriate the Sunday readings seem! Zechariah looks forward to a meek savior riding on an ass who will banish the trappings of war, chariot, and horse, and proclaim peace to the nations. In the gospel Jesus prays in gratitude to the Father for the gift of revelation to the "little ones" and then invites those who labor and are burdened to come to him, since he is meek and humble of heart. These hardly seem the attitudes and values so heralded today.

Because of the intimacy between Jesus and the Father, the gospel is often described as "a thunderbolt from the Johannine sky." It is also a virtual summary of Matthew's theology. Jesus is the one who reveals the very nature of God. He summons people to take up his yoke (an allusion to the Jewish use of taking on "the yoke of the Torah"), and as embodied wisdom he invites people to come to him (Matt 11:29). His self-revelation in Matthew is for the "little ones," people who are blessed at the beginning of his teaching (Matt 5:1-12) and who will carry his hidden presence at the final judgment (Matt 25:31-46).

These "little ones" are also those who labor and are burdened, a reference most likely to those who suffer under the burdens of religious obligations imposed by those who "tie up heavy burdens and lay them upon peoples' shoulders" (Matt 23:4), while neglecting the weightier things of the law such as "justice, mercy, and faith" (Matt 23:23, *au. trans.*). The "little ones" are also often those whose faith, when tested or fragile, is sustained by God. They are those who not only receive God's revelation but those who embody its deepest meaning for others.

In recent years the Church has been tested by scandal and leadership failures in a way never before known in its history on American soil. Yet where do we look for hope? I suggest we look to the "little ones" who have come to Jesus at times of trial. Recently I had ten African American students in a class on the Gospels. Throughout their lives they had taken on the yoke of Jesus and found rest. Now when many Catholics lack faith and trust in the institutional Church, such people are a beacon of hope. They never lost faith amid the discrimination and racism rampant in the churches. In spite of this, they hear the voice of Jesus summoning them to a deeper wisdom. I think also of generations of religious women, now aged, who taught and communicated the faith to first-generation immigrants, often themselves treated shabbily by the very institution they served. But they were really laboring on behalf of another group—God's "little ones."

In these continuing seasons of purification, when countless meetings and declarations of hierarchs ring hollow, Catholics must learn from the experience not only of Jesus, who was meek and humble of heart, but from those who cast their burdens on him. In a real sense then today, our countless civic celebrations are also celebrations of those little ones who came to this land fleeing persecution or seeking a decent life for their loved ones. Gospel and culture are a mandate for us to never forget to listen to the voices of the little ones who carry God's presence.

PRAYING WITH SCRIPTURE

- Recall your labors and burdens and place them before the risen Christ.

- Pray in remembrance and gratitude for those little ones who have received and lived the teaching of Jesus.

- The psalmist prays, "Every day will I bless you, Lord." Repeat this prayer while recalling God's blessings to you.

Fifteenth Sunday in Ordinary Time

Readings: Isa 55:10-11; Ps 65:10, 11, 12-13, 14; Rom 8:18-23; Matt 13:1-23

> **"We know that all creation is groaning in labor pains even until now" (Rom 8:22).**

DOWN ON THE FARM

Amos Wilder, whose New Testament scholarship spanned seven decades of the last century, wrote that in the parables the reader does not meet Jesus "the cloudy visionary" but the "layman" for whom human destiny is at stake in "ordinary creaturely existence, domestic, economic, social" (*Language of Gospel,* 82). Here the lives of ordinary people from a distant time and culture come alive in a way true of little ancient literature.

Jesus was familiar with a rural Galilean milieu: outdoor scenes of farming and shepherding, and domestic scenes in simple one-room houses (Luke 11:5-8). The homes of the rich are seen only through the kitchen door—the view of servants and slaves. The farming is hill-country farming, done in small patches with stone fences and briars (Mark 4:5-7), not that of the broad lowland plains. There are donkeys, sheep, wolves, and birds; seeds, wheat, and harvests; lilies of the field and fruit trees; patched wineskins and household lamps; children quarreling in the marketplace; and shady merchants. People are threatened by drought and flood, and the din of war is never distant. Jesus sees life through the eyes of the ʿanawîm, the poor and humble of the land.

The gospels for the next three weeks are from Jesus' sermon in parables, and through them we enter the world of first-century agriculture. The parable of the sower (really the different sowings) and its interpretation appear in the three Synoptic Gospels. The seed is sown in what seems a silly way—thrown on the ground and then plowed under. Not surprisingly, three-fourths of the seed that lands on a footpath, on rocky ground, and among thorns produces no grain. The surprise of the parable is that one-fourth of the seed produces truly extraordinary results, even to a hundredfold, far making up for the loss. Jesus wants his followers to know that God's kingdom is that way: extraordinary results from seeming failure.

Building on the image from Isaiah of the word of God as rain that nurtures a fruitful seed, Matthew wrestles with the failure of the word. In an extremely enigmatic set of sayings, Jesus quotes Isaiah to show that this failure is not due to God's word but arises from unwillingness to listen and be converted (Matt 13:13-15 = Isa 6:9-10). The interpretation of the sower (Matt 13:18-23) allegorizes the original parable of Jesus to describe ways in which followers of Jesus can fail by superficial acceptance of Jesus' teaching, by fear of persecution, and by the lure of riches and wealth. Yet the allegory equally assures Jesus' followers that the rich soil of hearing and understanding will produce astonishing results.

In the initial parable we are in touch not only with a Jesus who offers images of hope but who expresses his own hope as opposition mounts. As with Jesus and Paul (second reading), so for ourselves creation becomes a text that leads us deeper into the mysteries of God. In the allegory of the responses, even human failures will not overwhelm the power of God's word to take root in rich soil. Like all parables, these leave us with questions: As we look around our world, where can we find images and messages of hope amid repeated loss and ever-recurring human failure?

PRAYING WITH SCRIPTURE

- Pray over the ways in which God's word has taken root in your heart and brought forth a great harvest.

- Reflect on how "worldly anxiety and the lure of riches" often choke the word of God today.

- Contemplate ways in which nature speaks to you of God's action.

Sixteenth Sunday in Ordinary Time

Readings: Wis 12:13, 16-19; Ps 86:5-6, 9-10, 15-16; Rom 8:26-27;
Matt 13:24-43 [13:24-30]

"You, O Lord, are good and forgiving" (Ps 86:5).

HOW ODD OF GOD!

"This has got to stop!" "Why doesn't somebody do something about this?"—refrains heard from family kitchen, to recreation rooms of religious communities (perhaps more frequently). Jesus' followers were no different. Jesus again compares God's kingdom to the work of a sower who sows good seed, expecting a fine harvest. But an enemy comes and sows weeds with the wheat. The farm workers quite naturally urge the householder to root out the weeds immediately. Surprisingly, since in the previous parable the weeds choke the growth, the householder tells the workers to let them both grow together, because "you might uproot the wheat along with them." There will be time enough at the harvest to be sure of the difference. Matthew's allegorical application of this parable to his community (vv. 36-43) clearly identifies the wheat with the righteous and the weeds with evildoers and with those who cause others to sin.

Despite the desire of the disciples to know *right now* who are the good and who are the evildoers, Jesus says, "Just wait!" The community as it moves through history is composed of good and bad people but cannot always be sure who is who. Precipitous separation may destroy the good (the wheat) while trying to uproot the weeds.

This parable anticipates the following ones (mustard seed; leaven), where things are not always as they seem. The mustard seed is not only small, but it can be a terrific nuisance, since it produces a hearty bush that takes over where it is not wanted. Jesus says that God's "reigning" is this way; it may seem small and insignificant, but the birds of the sky nest in it. The bush with swarms of nesting birds is a sardonic allusion to Daniel 4:7-24, where the people of Nebuchadnezzar's kingdom nest

90

in the huge and mighty tree of his rule. No, for Jesus small seeds and mustard bushes are enough.

In the final parable for this Sunday, Jesus turns from the world of farming to women's work of preparing bread for the family. Similar motifs characterize both parables: hidden growth, contrast between insignificant beginnings (mustard seed, leaven) and astonishing results (enough bread for a hundred people). The choice of leaven for the action of God is surprising, for in the Bible, yeast is almost always a symbol of corruption or evil action (see Matt 16:5-7; 1 Cor 5:7-8).

These short but powerful parables tell us that "God's ways are not our ways" (Isa 55:8). We often would like God's reign to unfold in particular ways, perhaps by rooting out the weeds; hoping that it might be more powerful and visible, not some troublesome bush; anxious for visible signs of success; suspicious of "corrupting influences." An older Jesuit once told me that his father said to him when he was a little boy, "Harry, God is at times a mighty unpredictable fellow!" How true of the parables of Jesus; how often untrue in the minds of Jesus' followers then and now, who are quite sure they know God's will.

PRAYING WITH SCRIPTURE

• Quietly pray over the attributes of God in Psalm 86:15: "merciful and gracious, slow to anger, abounding in kindness and fidelity."

• When prayer seems impossible, recall Paul's words that "the Spirit comes to the aid of our weakness."

• Jesus images God's kingdom through a woman preparing bread. Pray over the ways in which women nourish the Church today.

Seventeenth Sunday in Ordinary Time

Readings: 1 Kgs 3:5, 7-12; Ps 119:57, 72, 76-77, 127-128, 129-130;
Rom 8:28-30; Matt 13:44-52

> **"We know that all things work for good**
> **for those who love God" (Rom 8:28).**

FINDERS KEEPERS!

This Sunday concludes Jesus' sermon in parables, with three kingdom parables and a covert reference to the evangelist Matthew. The kingdom, or better "God's way of reigning," is first compared to the joy of unexpected discovery of a treasure in a field, causing a person to sell everything and buy the field. Exegetes have filled volumes with "Jesuitical" attempts to absolve Jesus of counseling dishonesty, since the finder apparently should have told the owner of the treasure. Yet, Jesus seems less concerned than the scholars about skirting the law. He praises the chicanery of a person who juggles the books (Luke 16:1-8) and approves investing money at interest (Matt 25:14-30). He also manifests a penchant for associating with lowlifes—"a glutton and a drunkard, a friend of tax collectors and sinners" (Matt 11:19). The main point of the parable is *not* simply on the decision to sell everything to gain the treasure but on *the joy of discovery.* The treasure of God's forgiveness, when found in the proclamation of Jesus, releases hearers to respond without counting the cost.

The second parable of "finding" is somewhat different. Here a purposeful merchant has been looking perhaps all his life for a precious pearl, and when he comes across it, he sells all (no immorality here) to buy it. Though the joy of finding is presumed, the stress here is on the long and successful search. These two parables mirror people's experience of discovering God's love and forgiveness, perhaps unexpectedly, perhaps after a long search.

The third illustration, of the net hauling in good and bad fish. is really an allegory of the final judgment and corresponds to the interpretation of the weeds and wheat (Matt 13:36-43). Matthew thus brackets two parables of everyday experience with visions of the end time; these parables warn against a precipitous separation of the good from the evil, as well as a warning that the treasure and costly pearl of God's reign should evoke a response of grateful and faithful discipleship.

People of a certain age will remember how Alfred Hitchcock always appeared in a cameo role in his films. Matthew the evangelist makes such an appearance in the final verses of this chapter. He is the scribe trained for the kingdom of heaven who brings from his storeroom both the old and the new: stories and sayings that date back to the historical Jesus, combined with his own reflection and arrangement of this material to apply the gospel to new situations faced by his community. What a legacy for those who hand on the faith today!

PRAYING WITH SCRIPTURE

- Prayerfully think of ways in which "mustard seeds" are growing into mighty bushes in today's Church.

- Pray over times when we were all too willing to separate the good from the bad.

- Reflect on moments of joyful discovery of God's treasures and pearls.

Eighteenth Sunday in Ordinary Time

Readings: Isa 55:1-3; Ps 145; Rom 8:35, 37-39; Matt 14:13-21

> **"Heed me, and you shall eat well,**
> **you shall delight in rich fare" (Isa 55:2).**

SUMMER FARE!

Who forgot the mustard? Such pleas often punctuate summer cook-outs and picnics in the park. The gospel, though not exactly describing a picnic on the Galilean hills, tells of Jesus' meeting the needs of hungry followers.

Matthew establishes a rhythm of Jesus as Messiah in word and in deed. After engaging Jesus' teaching in parables, the gospels for the following three Sundays portray powerful works (miracles) of Jesus. The first of these is the miraculous feeding of the five thousand, one of the few miracles found in all four Gospels. The feeding is a "gift miracle," in which God, through a prophet, meets material needs in surprising ways (1 Kgs 17:8-16; 2 Kgs 4:42-44). Unlike other miracles where a request precedes the miracle, Jesus' action arises from his compassion for suffering people.

Though abbreviating Mark's account (6:30-44), distinctive Matthean emphases emerge. He omits Mark's challenge to Jesus by the disciples (6:30), portraying them rather as wondering how they will feed the people. This suggests the Matthean theme of "little faith," which is strengthened by Jesus (Matt 6:31; 8:26; 14:31). By explicitly stating that "it was evening" and by omitting the distribution of fish, Matthew heightens the connection with the Eucharist (Matt 26:20-29).

The readings provide rich fare for reflection and preaching. God is the one who summons the thirsty and hungry that they may have life (first reading). Jesus provides food out of compassion for suffering people—a mandate for a Church in a world of staggering hunger. The feast also recalls the banquet of "Lady Wisdom" (Prov 9:1-2), who provides spiritual nourishment to her disciples. The "deserted place" evokes memories of the manna given to a pilgrim people in their wilderness wanderings and anticipates the Eucharist as nurture for a pilgrim Church. The abundance of food is also a symbol of that messianic banquet, when death and hunger will no longer stalk our lives (Matt 26:28). A good menu for a summer picnic, but don't forget the seasonings.

PRAYING WITH SCRIPTURE

- When praying before meals, recall the number of times that Jesus ate with his disciples and fed the hungry.

- Pray for those groups like "Bread for the World," which are dedicated to countering hunger throughout the world.

- Repeat slowly the words of the opening prayer: "Our life is your gift. Guide our life's journey."

Nineteenth Sunday in Ordinary Time

Readings: 1 Kgs 19:9a, 11-13a; Ps 85:9, 10, 11-12, 13-14; Rom 9:1-5;
Matt 14:22-33

"Take courage, it is I; do not be afraid" (Matt 14:27).

That Sinking Feeling!

Peter is more prominent in Matthew's Gospel than in any other. Along with Matthew 16:16-19 (the promise to Peter) and 17:24-27 (the Temple tax), today's gospel is one of three distinctive Petrine episodes. Through-out these, Peter's faith is a gift from God that is tested by suffering and doubt, only to be strengthened by Jesus. Like many of Jesus' most strik-ing acts of power, today's story is a narrative of a "sea rescue" (see Matt 8:23-27; John 6:16-21), which also reflects the Old Testament motif of God as one who controls the power of the raging sea and the chaos mon-sters that lurk there (Pss 42:7-8; 65:8; 89:10; 107:23-32).

Matthew appends the Petrine incident to his Markan source (Mark 6:45-52). Jesus appears to the storm-tossed disciples with the words, "take courage, it is I (Greek, *egō eimi*, the divine revelatory formula); do not be afraid. " But, with typical bravado, Peter tests Jesus saying, "Lord, if it is you, command me to come to you on the water." Leaving the boat Peter immediately sinks, only to cry out, "save me," which Jesus does while rebuking him for his little faith, which then evokes Peter's confession, "Truly, you are the Son of God."

Though Catholics naturally think of Peter as "the first bishop of Rome," and the pope as "the vicar of Peter," in Matthew, he is a model for *all* of Christ's followers. He is called by Christ but suffers from un-certainty and doubt throughout his life, only to fail and deny Jesus dur-ing the Passion. Yet at each stage he is rescued or strengthened by Jesus, and in contrast to Mark, is one of the disciples to whom the risen Jesus appears. Far from a symbol of certainty and unyielding fidelity, Peter in Matthew is a symbol for a pilgrim church that often misunderstands Jesus, struggles with doubt, often with "little faith," and even abandons Jesus in time of trial. Yet Jesus appears with the words "fear not," a message which the present successor to Peter, Pope John Paul II, uttered when elected and which he continues to proclaim.

PRAYING WITH SCRIPTURE

- Follow the example of Paul, who prays in gratitude for his Jewish heritage, by thinking of the gifts that Judaism brings to people today.

- At times of "little faith," repeat softly the words of Jesus: "Take courage, it is I; do not be afraid."

- Elijah does not hear the voice of God in the wind, the falling mountains, or the fire, but in a "tiny whispering sound." Where do we hear God's "whispers" today?

Twentieth Sunday in Ordinary Time

Readings: Isa 56:1, 6-7; Ps 67:2-3, 5, 6, 8; Rom 11:13-15, 29-32;
Matt 15:21-28

"O woman, great is your faith!" (Matt 15:28).

MOTHER COURAGE!

Though Matthew stresses that the primary mission of Jesus was to the "house of Israel," in today's gospel a non-Jewish woman draws him to a more universalistic vision. Narrated by both Mark (7:24-30) and Matthew, this story of courageous faith and boundary-crossing challenges the Church today.

The woman is a Canaanite, a term evoking Israel's ancient enemies, who comes alone to Jesus, crying, "Have pity (or better, "mercy") on me Lord, Son of David!" which suggests that she had heard of his healing power. Since illness was thought to arise from demonic attack, she begs release and healing for her daughter. Jesus meets her request with stony silence, and the disciples say, "Get rid of her, for she keeps yelling at us" *(au. trans.)*. Again Jesus rebuffs her: "I was sent only to the lost sheep of the house of Israel." In no other miracle story has a petitioner been treated so harshly.

The narrative changes when the woman, doubly an outsider—a Gentile and alone in public—challenges this rebuff by "worshiping" Jesus (something no disciple does prior to the resurrection) and uttering the simple prayer, "Lord, help me." Again a rebuff from Jesus, harsher than the earlier two: "It is not right to take the food of the children (Jews) and throw it to the dogs" (Gentiles). Not to be put off, the woman turns Jesus' words back on him: "Please, Lord," jokingly calling herself "a puppy" (in Greek), asks for the crumbs that fall from the table. In a startling turn of events, Jesus replies, "O woman, great is your faith! Let it be done for you as you wish," and her daughter is healed at that moment.

Two interpretations have accompanied this narrative throughout history. Building on the first reading, where the Gentiles will come to Israel's

God to form a house of prayer for all nations, the Canaanite woman is a symbol of those nations that will hear the message of the gospel. The courageous faith of the woman is a second major theme.

But neither of these themes captures the parabolic surprise of the narrative. The woman's brash courage actually "converts" Jesus. Twice in Matthew, Jesus has limited his mission to the sons and daughters of Israel (Matt 10:5-6; 15:24). Yet here he crosses this self-imposed boundary to bring merciful healing to a Gentile. The woman brings him to the full implications of his mission. Today the deepest meaning of the gospel is often disclosed by the courage of an "outsider" who is driven by loving concern for innocent victims of disease or injustice. Often they have been met by stony silence or rude rebuff by Jesus' followers. The "great faith" of this mother, who breaks all boundaries out of love, is a model and challenge for our time.

PRAYING WITH SCRIPTURE

- When prayers seem unheard, recall in prayer the courage and persistence of the Canaanite woman.

- In times of crisis ask God for the gift of "great faith."

- Prayerfully recall those whose faith has led them to cross boundaries that separate people.

The Assumption of the Blessed Virgin Mary

Since this feast falls on a Monday, it is not a holy day of obligation.

Readings: Rev 11:19; 12:1-6; 10; Ps 45; 1 Cor 15:20-27; Luke 1:39-56

"My soul proclaims the greatness of the Lord" (Luke 1:39).

CLOTHED WITH THE SUN

Marian feasts season the liturgical calendar as the Assumption falls in the middle of Ordinary Time. Though rooted in ancient tradition, especially the Eastern tradition of the "Dormition of Mary," this celebration, unlike the Annunciation, the Visitation, and Our Lady of Sorrows, has no explicit scriptural basis. Yet the readings lead us more deeply into the mystery of Mary's role in salvation history. In profoundly allegorical language, the book of Revelation envisions a queen of the universe, clothed with the sun, standing on the moon, with a crown of twelve stars. In intense labor, this woman (in context, a symbol of Israel) will bring forth a messiah who will be persecuted by worldly powers. For centuries the Church has appropriated this woman as Mary, the new Eve, who now reigns with the Messiah (Christ).

The gospel portrays an earthly woman about to give birth who sings in joy of God's greatness and goodness to her people, Israel. Like the prophets of old, Mary speaks on behalf of the lowly and heralds God's judgment on the rich and powerful. Appropriate to today's feast is Mary's prediction that "from this day all generations will call me blessed: the Almighty has done great things for me." Among the *magnalia Dei* ("great deeds of God") is the assumption of Mary "body and soul into heaven." In many of the beautiful icons of the Dormition of Mary, she is pictured in death surrounded by the disciples, as Jesus carries her "soul" to heaven in the form of an infant.

But essential to the Assumption is the word "body." In the words of the dogmatic definition, "the ever Virgin Mary, having completed the course of her earthly life, was assumed body and soul into heavenly glory" (Pius XII, Nov. 1, 1950). The dogma arose from centuries of reflection on the relation of Mary to the total Christ-event. The readings today capture this. Paul looks to the transformation of all in Christ and to the resurrection of their bodies. Today's feast says that Mary now lives with that transformation that is our hope.

As the body is the bearer and symbol of the person in this life, so too will it remain when all are brought to life in Christ (1 Cor 15:22). Sister Mary Aquin O'Neil, R.S.M., theologian and director of the Mount St. Agnes Theological Center for Women (Baltimore), sees this as crucial for women today and for all of theology. Mary's bodily assumption is a corrective to any misogny that views the female body as a source of defilement or evil (for example, 1 Tim 2:9-15). Woman's body carried Christ in her womb; woman's body reigns in glory.

PRAYING WITH SCRIPTURE

- Read prayerfully Mary's *Magnificat* (Luke 1:46-55), pausing with prayers of gratitude and petition to Mary.

- Ask Mary to grant our culture an appreciation of the dignity of the human body.

- Repeat softly the words of the opening prayer of the Mass: "May the prayers of this woman clothed with the sun bring Jesus to the waiting world."

Twenty-First Sunday in Ordinary Time

Readings: Isa 22:19-23; Ps 138:1-2, 2-3, 6, 8; Rom 11:33-36;
Matt 16:13-20

> **"You are Peter, and upon this rock
> I will build my church" (Matt 16:18).**

CHECKING THE FOUNDATION

If there is one New Testament passage that seems to define Catholicism, it is the Petrine promise of Matthew 16:16-20. Matthew supplements Peter's confession that Jesus is the Christ (Mark 8:29) by the more solemn affirmation "You are the Christ, *the Son of the living God*" and adds extraordinary statements about Peter. He is "blessed" because he, like the "little ones" of Matthew 11:25, has been gifted with divine revelation and receives a new mission, symbolized by the name change. Simon, son of Jonah, becomes Peter, the rock (Greek: *petros*) on which Jesus will build his Church, which the power of evil cannot surmount ("gates of the underworld").

Like the steward Eliakim in Isaiah, who receives symbols of power and the key of the house of David, Peter will receive the keys of the kingdom and is given the power to bind and to loose, which will be ratified in heaven. Somewhat paradoxically, having altered Mark to enhance the role of Peter, Matthew leaves virtually intact the subsequent misunderstanding of Peter, whom Jesus rebukes as a "Satan," who "is not thinking as God does, but as humans do." Matthew also brackets the Petrine blessing and promise with two special additions of Jesus rescuing a presumptuous Peter from drowning (14:28-32) and later teaching an obtuse Peter about the freedom of the sons of the kingdom (17:24-27).

Throughout history this Petrine promise has been interpreted in different ways. In Matthew, Peter is the model disciple who must be constantly sustained by Christ, and in the early Church he is remembered primarily as an apostle and martyr. The typological interpretation is very early and called "the mother" of the other interpretations: Peter is the type of every true, spiritual Christian on whom the Church is built (Origen, *Comm. in Matt.*,12:10). The "Eastern" interpretation is that the rock is the faith of Peter, so that the Church is built on the faith of believing Christians, and strong in the Middle Ages is the Christological interpretation where Christ is the rock (see 1 Cor 3:11; 10:4). An interpretation dating from the fourth century is the Roman/pontifical interpretation. The rock is Peter, and promises to Peter extend to successors in Petrine ministry, which, since the First Vatican Council, is normative for Roman Catholics. Fundamental to all interpretations and to the Johannine version of the Petrine promise (John 21:15-19) are Jesus' words that the Church is my Church and the sheep *my* sheep. Ultimately, faith rests on Christ, who is the Good Shepherd of the flock.

Since Vatican I the papacy has achieved an authority and influence never before seen in Church history. In an often chaotic century, the centralized papacy has offered a prophetic voice against evil and injustice, and fostered the unity and the spread of the Church, often, though, at the price of unproductive centralization. While the influence of Matthew 16:13-20 is clear in the exercise of the papal office, it is difficult to see how Matthew 18:18, where the power to bind and loose is given to the whole Church, has shaped the episcopacy and the wider community of disciples.

Still, ecumenical dialogues with both the traditional Churches of the East and those stemming from the Reformation are now exploring ways in which a Petrine ministry might function in a renewed Church. In his encyclical on ecumenism (*Ut Unum Sint*, 1995), Pope John Paul II notes challenges arising from the Petrine office and asks Orthodox and Protestants to join with him to envision the kind of papacy that could serve Christian unity in the future. This new vision may be shaped by courageous voices from the margin, not unlike that of the Canaanite woman (Matt 15:22).

PRAYING WITH SCRIPTURE

- Pray for the kind of "Petrine ministry" envisioned by Pope John Paul II.

- Continue to pray that the Church not lose heart in overcoming religious division.

- Among different images of Jesus alive today, think often of how you respond to Jesus' question to Peter: "But who do you say that I am?"

Twenty-Second Sunday in Ordinary Time

Readings: Jer 20:7-9; Ps 63:2, 3-4, 5-6, 8-9; Rom 12:1-2;
Matt 16:21-27

"You are thinking not as God does,
but as human beings do" (Matt 16:23).

A Shifting Rock

After the grand promises given to Peter in Matthew 16:16-20, Jesus points his disciples to Jerusalem, where he will suffer greatly and ultimately be crucified. Peter, to whom God revealed that Jesus was the Messiah, "rebukes" Jesus (a strong word, used often when Jesus "rebukes" a demon), saying, "God forbid, Lord! No such thing shall ever happen to you." In language used against no other disciple, Jesus calls Peter "Satan" (in the original sense of "adversary" rather than demon) and says that he is an "obstacle." This is a weak translation of the Greek *skandalon* (literally a "snare"), often used with the word "stone," which trips a person or causes him or her to fall (Rom 9:33; 1 Pet 2:8). What a transformation from the rock on which Jesus will build his Church!

The next section of the gospel captures the theme of the liturgy: the cost of hearing and following God's word. In the first reading Jeremiah, who was hated and persecuted by kings and other prophets, laments his very call. God has "duped" him, a word often used of sexual seduction, and he says to himself that he will no more mention God or speak in God's name. Yet he cannot abandon his prophetic mission, which is a fire burning in his heart, imprisoned in his bones. This burning fire will only fuel more hatred and suffering.

All Jesus' followers are summoned to deny themselves and to be ready to follow Jesus by taking up their cross, "for whoever wishes to save his [or her] life, will lose it, but whoever loses his [or her] life for my sake will find it" (gospel). Taking up the cross and denying one's self captures the paradoxical ethics of Matthew's Gospel. The "life" promised to disciples is the true life embodied and taught by Jesus: rejection

104

of power when offered all the kingdoms of the world; a paradoxical identification with the poor, the mourners, the peacemakers, and those who seek justice; forgiveness of enemies; quiet and constant prayer to a loving Father; inner peace amid threats and suffering—all these are thinking as God thinks.

"Denying one's self" is more profound than daily acts of "mortification." It means displacing one's self from the center of our consciousness while looking to the true self embodied by Jesus' teaching. The self that is lost is the autonomous individual so dear to American consciousness. The self that is found is true life in a community of brothers and sisters who take up the challenge of discipleship by speaking and living from the fire that burns within their hearts. Such discipleship embodies a life of costly grace described by Dietrich Bonhoeffer, who carried his cross to death in opposing Nazism. He described costly grace as "the gospel which must be sought again and again, the gift which must be asked for . . . such grace is costly because it calls us to follow, and it is grace because it calls us to follow Jesus Christ. It is costly because it costs him his life, and it is grace because it gives a man the only true life." Peter, firm rock and stumbling stone, learned this only after he failed and even denied Jesus.

PRAYING WITH SCRIPTURE

- Ask God for the grace that leads you to know your true self and what must be denied to find this self.

- When the prospect of suffering looms, think of Jesus who had "to suffer greatly."

- Pray in gratitude for those Christians today who model heroic discipleship amid persecution and even death.

Twenty-Third Sunday in Ordinary Time

Readings: Ezek 33:7-9; Ps 95:1-2, 6-7, 8-9; Rom 13:8-10;
Matt 18:15-20

"Love is the fulfillment of the law" (Rom 13:10).

TOUGH LOVE!

Since the public revelation of the sex abuse scandal in January 2002, much of Church life has been dominated by reports of shameful actions by its priests and hierarchy, and continues to be preoccupied (although belatedly) with protecting its most vulnerable members. The fourth of the great discourses of Jesus in Matthew (ch. 18), called "the sermon on the Church," addresses similar issues: concern for the vulnerable, confronting sin, and forgiveness.

The chapter begins with a typical dispute among Jesus' disciples over "who is the greatest" (18:1-9). Jesus calls a child, sets it down in the middle of them, and says that unless they become like this child, they will not enter the kingdom of heaven, for whoever humbles himself like the child will be "the greatest." You can hear the gasp of the disciples across the centuries. Children were not symbols of innocence nor the endearing nucleus of a family, but symbols of powerlessness who required the care and protection of others. Jesus then continues with dire warnings against those who become stumbling blocks to one of "these little ones who believe in me." The ground has shifted a bit, since such little ones are also the vulnerable members of the community who have "little faith." Rather than becoming a snare for such people, a person should choose self-mutilation.

Matthew's concern for the weakest members of the community emerges in the following parable of the lost sheep (18:10-14). One sheep wanders off (a term used normally for moral straying), and the shepherd leaves the ninety-nine on the mountain to seek the errant member. The most vulnerable becomes the criterion of pastoral care. This seems like a strange way to care for the welfare of a community.

Today's gospel seems to present a different way of dealing with sinners. First there is a one-to-one confrontation, followed by a meeting with official witnesses, and then an appearance before the "church" (assembly of believers). If the sinner persists, he is to be treated as a "Gentile or tax collector," a decision that will be ratified by God. Clearly Matthew, like Paul, was faced with situations in which a particular member was a threat to the good of the community (see also 1 Cor 5:1-8). In this passage, which deals with the unity and reconciliation of differences in the community, the power of binding and loosing earlier given to Peter (Matt 16:19) is granted to the whole community of disciples.

This is a classic instance of Matthew's bringing out from his "storeroom both the new and the old," (13:52) and changing traditional teaching by placement of material. This disciplinary teaching is sandwiched between the parable of the lost sheep (the errant brother or sister is sought out rather than thrown out) and that of the unmerciful servant, next week's gospel (where Peter is counseled to have unlimited forgiveness). The tension between Church order and the example of Christ remains through the ages.

Yet, from the perspective of the whole Gospel, dealing with the sinner as a tax collector and Gentile may not be so harsh. Jesus heals the servant of a Gentile tax collector (8:5-13), while a slur against Jesus is that he is "a glutton and a drunkard, a friend of tax collectors and sinners." When the ordinary ecclesial structures of reconciliation break down, the true shepherd must seek the one who is lost. Treating a sinner like the Gentile or tax collector is not simply to practice *excommunication* but to seek new ways of *communication*.

Praying with Scripture

- Pray over ways that your parish or community may strive to resolve conflict.

- Paul writes to the Romans, "Owe nothing to anyone, except to love one another." What debts of love do you owe to others?

- Repeat the phrase from the opening prayer: "Lord, our God, in you justice and mercy meet."

Twenty-Fourth Sunday in Ordinary Time

Readings: Sir 27:30–28:7; Ps 103:1-2, 3-4, 9-10, 11-2; Rom 14:7-9; Matt 18:21-35

> **"He pardons all your iniquities, heals all your ills"**
> **(Ps 103:3).**

STAYING OUT OF PRISON

Following the law of "end stress," Matthew's sermon on Church life concludes with a dramatic parable that shapes the interpretation of the whole chapter. Peter provides the foil for Jesus' teaching by asking how often he must forgive a sinning brother or sister, suggesting a limit of seven times. Jesus counters with a call for limitless forgiveness and then tells him a parable that does not really answer Peter's question about the quantity of forgiveness but images its precondition. The parable falls into three acts.

Act One: The narrative begins somewhat ominously with a king "auditing the books," then summoning one of his debtors for an accounting, evoking much the same reaction as a dinnertime message today: "Honey, there is a man from the IRS on the phone." The man owes ten thousand talents; the translation "huge amount" is particularly inadequate, since the debt constituted more than the yearly taxes collected from the Roman province of Asia. (Before Enron and WorldCom, I thought this was utterly unrealistic.) When the debt could not be repaid, the king orders him and his family sold into slavery. As a last ditch chance, the debtor begs the king to give him time to repay the loan, but surprisingly "out of compassion," the king forgave the debt. If the parable ended here, it would be a wonderful story of God's limitless compassion and forgiveness.

Act Two: The forgiven debtor rushes out to tell his family the good news, only to run into a "fellow servant" who owed him "a much smaller amount," one hundred denarii, that is, roughly a third of a year's wage. Matthew's readers, recalling Jesus' response to Peter, might expect that the first servant would cancel the debt and embrace his fellow debtor. Shockingly, he rather grabs him by the throat and throws him into debtor's prison.

Act Three: At this point the sympathy of the hearers shifts from rejoicing with the first servant to seeing him as a moral monster in his treatment of a fellow debtor. Other servants who are "deeply disturbed" go immediately to the king and report the gross injustice. The king, who was initially a model of compassion, now exercises justice for the sake of the powerless victim. His words are the key to the parable: "Should you not have had mercy on your fellow servant, as I had mercy on you?" (18:33, *au. trans.;* the Lectionary translation "pity" for "mercy" is poor).

The original debtor's actions seem totally incomprehensible and ultimately self-destructive. How could he act this way? His original request is a clue. He is faced with an unpayable debt but does not ask that it be forgiven, but only "Be patient with me, and I will pay you back in full." The king does not grant his request but forgives the debt. The soon to be unforgiving servant wants to restore the order of strict justice but receives mercy. When he meets his fellow servant, the servant addresses him in the same words he spoke to the king, "Be patient with me, and I will pay you back." His previous way of viewing the world in terms of rights and duties come screaming back. The mercy and forgiveness that he received were something that simply "happened" to him, not an extraordinary event that changed his way of viewing the world.

Jesus applies the parable to Peter's question, saying, "So will my heavenly Father do to you, unless each of you forgives your brother [or sister] from *your heart.* What is called for is a totally new way of viewing the world—*metanoia* (Matt 4:17), a change of heart. God who comes to expression in Matthew's parables desires "mercy [NAB: "love"] not sacrifice" (Hos 6:6, see Matt 9:13; 12:7) and summons people to be forgiving because they have experienced forgiveness. This parable cautions against a legalistic or closed way of experiencing life that filters the unexpected through the narrow categories of rights and duties.

As the conclusion to the sermon on the Church and in response to Peter's questions, the parable states that all Church order is subject to the law of mercy and forgiveness. Only those who have experienced mercy and forgiveness can mediate this to others. The power of "binding and loosing" can be exercised only by those who have experienced God's compassionate and undeserved mercy and learn to forgive a brother or sister from their hearts.

PRAYING WITH SCRIPTURE

• Pray over those times in which you have imitated the first servant.

- Place before God what you feel may be "unpayable debts"
- Read prayerfully Psalm 103, a hymn of praise for God's compassionate goodness.

Twenty-Fifth Sunday in Ordinary Time

Readings: Isa 55:6-9; Ps 145:2-3, 8-9, 17-18; Phil 1:20c-24, 27a;
Matt 20:1-16a

> **"As high as the heavens are above the earth,**
> **so high are my ways above your ways" (Isa 55:9).**

NO FAIR!

Two attitudes vie for center stage in American life. One is a great sense
of fairness and concern for equal rights, "equal pay for equal work,"
"equal opportunity for all;" the other, a concern for the underdog; a joy
when the last become first; the small college upsetting a national power
on an autumn afternoon; the Florida Marlins triumphing over the mighty
Yankees in the "Fall classic"— rags-to-riches success stories. Today's
gospel seems to challenge fairness at the expense of concern for the "last."

Though called the parable of the vineyard workers, the central character is really the landowner, who appears at axial moments in the story
and determines its shape. In a scene not unlike the stirring images from
On the Waterfront, day laborers are lined up waiting for work, most likely
as the harvest season draws to a close. The landowner offers them the
usual daily wage (a denarius), and happily they go off to work. Then a
strange sequence unfolds. He goes out again at nine, noon, and three in
the afternoon and hires more for a wage simply called "just." More surprisingly, he goes out near the end of the work day, finds straggling
would-be workers and hires them (with no stipulated salary). At this
point the parable is about a surprisingly generous landowner. Jesus' hearers might think of a bountiful God always ready to share his goodness.

The mood shifts dramatically when payment time comes. Not the
owner but his foreman is told somewhat illogically to distribute the
wages, "beginning with the last and ending with the first" (the twelve-
hour workers). This is an instance of the power of the parables to orient
by disorienting. When the realism of the parable breaks down, the deeper
meaning of the parable emerges. Those who had barely worked up a

sweat receive a denarius, and we can almost hear the rest of the workers chatting approvingly in the hope of receiving more. Yet each received the same daily wage.

Their anticipated joy turned immediately to grumbling: "These last ones worked only one hour, and you have made them equal to us, who bore the day's burden and the heat." The generous and good landowner now seems to be both legalistic and arbitrary, saying that he did them "no injustice" (more accurate than "not cheating" in the Lectionary) and that he can do with his resources what he wants.

Does this parable summon us to simply stand in awe with Isaiah over the mysterious ways of God? Yet the surprise of the parable is provocative today. Essential to its interpretation is that the order of justice is maintained; the grumbling workers received what they agreed upon. Justice provides the background against which goodness can appear as true goodness. The grumblers' complaint is not simply economic, but *"you have made them equal to us."* They are defining their personal worth in contrast to others and are not so much angered by what happened to them as envious of the good fortune of others. They are so enclosed in their understanding of justice that it alone becomes the norm by which they relate to others and want to order the world by their norms, which limit the landowner's freedom and exclude startling generosity.

The final words of the owner unmask their deeper problem: "Are you envious because I am generous" (literally: "Is your eye evil because I am good?"). In Matthew "the lamp of the body is the eye" (6:22), which should be plucked out if it causes one to sin (5:29). The attitude of the grumbling servants distorts their view the world. When envy poisons a person's perception, an act of goodness and generosity to others blinds people to their own and others' good fortune.

The parable summons us to believe that God's justice played out in this world is not limited by human conceptions of strict mathematical judgment, where reward is in proportion to effort or merit. Mercy and goodness challenge us, as they did the workers in the parable, to move beyond justice, even though they do not exist at the expense of justice. God's ways are not human ways. Categories of worth and value by which humans separate themselves from others are reversed in God's eyes. When divine freedom is limited by human conceptions of God's goodness, men and women may never be able to experience undeserved goodness. Not to rejoice in the benefits given to others is to cut ourselves off from those benefits we have received. Our eyes, too, become evil.

PRAYING WITH SCRIPTURE

• With the grumbling workers, place your complaints before God.

- Pray over times when you have felt resentful over the goodness given to others, and think of ways that God has been gracious and merciful toward you (Ps 145:8).

- Think of ways that justice in our society must be transformed by generosity.

Twenty-Sixth Sunday in Ordinary Time

Readings: Ezek 18:25-28; Ps 25:4-5, 6-7, 8-9; Phil 2:1-11;
Matt 21:28-32

> **"Your ways, O Lord, make known to me;**
> **teach me your paths" (Ps 25:4).**

THE GOOD SON

For the next three weeks our tour through Matthew's storehouse of things old and things new (Matt 13:52) pauses at three parables, often called "Matthew's debate with the synagogue across the street." They are told amid the mounting opposition to Jesus during his final days in Jerusalem but are strongly influenced by the struggle for Jewish identity between the emerging Christian group and the nascent rabbinic movement after the destruction of the Temple (A.D. 70).

Stories of two sons are a staple of Jewish tradition (for example, Esau and Jacob) and of the teaching of Jesus (see Luke 15:11-32). A man orders one son to work in the vineyard; he says "I will not," but has a change of heart and goes to work. The other son immediately says yes but never ends up in the vineyard. The parable leaves us wondering what the father would do. What happens to the deceptive son? But Jesus interrupts with a question: "Which of the two did his father's will?" Jesus' adversaries, the chief priests and elders, are trapped, as was David by Nathan's parable (2 Sam 12:5). They must answer "the first"; then Jesus hammers home the application that while notorious sinners (original naysayers to God's commands) repented when they heard the teaching of John, the religious establishment did not, even when they saw the conversion of the tax collectors and prostitutes.

Matthew does not simply bash the Jewish leaders of Jesus' time but warns his own community. One indication is the question "Which of the two did his father's will?" "Will of the father" occurs elsewhere, always in the context of Jesus' instruction *of disciples* (6:10; 7:21; 12:50; 18:14), and Jesus' own prayer is that he do the Father's will (26:42). The parable contrasts a son who says, "Yes, sir (Greek: *kyrie*)" with the one who actually does the Father's will. At the conclusion of the Sermon on the Mount, this attitude distinguishes true disciples from false disciples: "Not everyone who says to me 'Lord, Lord,' will enter the kingdom of heaven, but only the one who does the will of my Father in heaven" (7:21). Jesus goes on to say that neither charismatic power nor proper theology is enough without bearing fruit or doing God's will.

Matthew's community is to imitate the "good son." It, too, is composed of people who like Peter said no, perhaps by denying Christ at times of persecution, but who turned and were transformed by God's grace. Matthew's community is not the heir of powerful religious leaders who prided themselves on their honorific titles and stunning interpretations of Torah, but of tax collectors, parade members of occupations forbidden to observant Jews, and women so oppressed that they sell their very selves. These kinds of people say yes and become "doers" of God's will.

The second reading provides the Christological foundation of such conversion. Jesus himself is the truly obedient Son who says yes to his Father in the most radical way. The initial verses of the hymn from Philippians explode with verbs of "doing." Jesus did not grasp at equality with God but emptied himself; he took on the form of a slave, he came in human likeness, he was obedient to the point of a criminal's death. The verbs then shift. God is now the "doer" by exalting Jesus and giving him a name above every name, the very name of the vineyard owner in Matthew (*kyrios* = lord). This is the attitude of Christ Jesus that true followers of Jesus are to adopt.

Matthew's application of the parable to his community has special power today. Both perennial and recent problems summon the Church to a depth of integrity that is expressed in deeds, not fine words. The Church is also always a community of forgiven sinners, even as today "unforgivable sins" seem to mount. The charter of the U.S. bishops against sex abuse, while filled with genuine concern for God's little ones, was a necessary but long-delayed response to a pervasive scandal. It was quickly followed by a pogrom on priests, many aged, and many no longer a threat to young people. How will this be reconciled with the picture of Jesus, the good Son, who not only warned against scandalizing the little ones (Matt 18:1-9) but was also called "a glutton and a drunkard, a friend of tax collectors and sinners" (Matt 11:19)?

PRAYING WITH SCRIPTURE

• Pray over times when you have said yes to God's call, only to falter when carrying it out.

- Pray over times when your initial no was transformed into a new way of following Christ.

- Pray over Paul's exhortation to his community not to look to their own interests but to the good of others (Phil 2:4).

Twenty-Seventh Sunday in Ordinary Time

*Readings: Isa 5:1-7; Ps 80:9, 12, 13-14, 15-16, 19-20; Phil 4:6-9;
Matt 21:33-43*

> **"Let me now sing of my friend,
> my friend's song concerning his vineyard" (Isa 5:1).**

"LOVE'S LABOR LOST"

Tales of unrequited love have shaped the tragic imagination in dramas: Euripides' *Medea*; Shakespeare's *Othello*, where the spurned Rodergio hastens the downfall of "one that loved not wisely, but too well"; epic poems with Dido on the shores of Carthage as Aeneas sails away; and the haunting arias of Bizet's *Carmen*. The real-life tragedy of spurned love plays out in divorce and family courts across the land.

The Bible itself offers a startling panorama of spurned love. "The God of Abraham, the God of Isaac, the God of Jacob" hears the complaints of his people against Egyptian slave drivers and knows their sufferings, comes down to rescue them, and makes with them a covenant of enduring fidelity (Exod 3:4-9). Then rhythms of failure and apostasy unfold, followed again and again by a rejected and suffering God reaching out to an obtuse people.

Isaiah's Song of the Vineyard (5:1-7) is a poignant reminder of such love. God, the friend, plants and constructs a vineyard with loving care so that it would yield fruit, but what came forth were "wild grapes." A distraught God pleads with the vineyard keepers, the inhabitants of Jerusalem and the people of Judah, "What more was there to do for my vineyard that I had not done?" Here the song turns tragic as God will cause ruin to the vineyard because he looked for judgment *(mishpat)* but received bloodshed *(mishpach)*, for justice *(sedaqah)* but received a cry *(seᶜaqah)*. Behind this threat stands the unjust exploitation of God's people by the Jerusalem aristocracy.

Today's gospel, named somewhat inaccurately the parable of the wicked tenants, is a virtual midrash, or commentary, on Isaiah's song.

The plot is deceptively simple. A man constructs a vineyard, reflecting God's care in Isaiah 5. He leases the vineyard to others and then wants his share of the produce. He sends three servants, whom the tenants rough up and kill, followed by another set more numerous than the first, who are treated the same—a bad lot, these tenants. Then, with seemingly obtuse logic, he muses that if he sends his son they will respect him. Not surprisingly, the tenants see this as an act of powerless desperation and kill the son. As in Isaiah, the mood shifts; the owner will come, "put those wretched men to a wretched death," and give the vineyard to others who will produce fruit.

In all the Gospels the parable becomes an allegory of the rejection of Jesus by the Jerusalem establishment, which results in the destruction of the Temple and the transfer of the vineyard to other tenants. Unfortunately this interpretation has fostered anti-Semitism throughout the ages. From the lips of the historical Jesus the parable may have had a more fundamental meaning. The utterly illogical action of the owner in sending the son reflects that pattern in which a long-suffering and compassionate God reaches out in the face of the most blatant forms of apostasy and idolatry (see also Hos 11–12). This parable expresses what Abraham Joshua Heschel has called "the divine pathos," which is the great paradox of biblical faith—a longing God's pursuit of humanity (*God in Search of Man,* p. 136). Jesus, who later laments over Jerusalem (Matt 23:37-39), brings to expression this shocking side of God's love, a love that will ultimately spell his own death. A better title for today's gospel might be "The Long-Suffering God."

Matthew does not revel in the destruction of the wicked tenants but turns their fate back on his hearers. The evil of the earlier tenants was not bearing fruit, yet Matthew stresses twice that these new tenants must bear fruit. Matthew's emerging Jewish Christian community is to look to its Jewish heritage not only as a warning but as guidance for its life. Isaiah summoned the earlier tenants to justice and righteousness by learning to do well, redressing the wronged, hearing the orphan's plea, and defending the widow (Isa 1:16-17). Those who do not bear fruit in things such as purity of heart and action, forgiveness and love of the enemy, and almsgiving for the needy will hear the ominous words of Jesus, "I never knew you. Depart from me, your evildoers" (Matt 7:23).

The readings today reenact on a divine scale the age-old mystery of total love given to another, which should blossom forth in bountiful fruit, but which, when refused or abused, unravels in destructive tragedy. The gospel calls on Christians today to think of themselves as gifted tenants of God's vineyard, while warning them of the consequences of neglect. It may be the season for the Church to review its agricultural practices.

PRAYING WITH SCRIPTURE

- Join in a prayer of lament with God over contemporary rejection of divine love and mercy.

- Repeat often the opening prayer of the liturgy, "Father, your love for us surpasses all our hopes and desires."

- Read prayerfully today's selection from Philippians as a picture of a community "bearing fruit."

Twenty-Eighth Sunday in Ordinary Time

Readings: Isa 25:6-10a; Ps 23:1-3a, 3b-4, 5, 6; Phil 4:12-14, 19-20; Matt 22:1-14

> **"The Lord God will wipe away the tears from every face" (Isa 25:8).**

What Shall I Wear to the Wedding?

Weddings have been a favorite theme in films in recent years, with titles such as *Bombay Wedding*, *A Polish Wedding*, and the spectacularly successful *My Big Fat Greek Wedding*, a film filled with the exuberant joy of the human condition and culminating in a wedding feast, with steaming plates of food, much to drink, and enthusiastic dancing. This reminded me of how frequently in literature and drama weddings are the setting for both a joyful denouement when young lovers surmount numerous hurdles on the road to the altar, as well as for the finale of an unfolding tragedy. So too in the Bible. Isaiah chooses the image of a feast of rich food and fine wines, where God will destroy death and wipe away every tear as he invites all nations to the table. When envisioning how God's reign will culminate at the end of history, Jesus tells of a king hosting a great wedding feast for his son.

In the first century a dual invitation was customary. Guests were invited well in advance and again gathered when the feast was about to begin. The banquet is prepared, everything is ready, and the king, perhaps somewhat satisfied, summons the guests. Shockingly, some simply ignore the invitation; others head out of town, and "the rest" beat up and killed the king's messengers. The generous host becomes the spurned "godfather" and sends his armies to wipe out the invited guests. Far from sulking, though, he orders other servants to go to the highways and byways and invite everyone they see, both the good and the bad.

Matthew, Luke, and the second-century Gospel of Thomas recount this parable with very different applications. In Luke, the substitute guests are "the poor, the crippled, the blind and the lame," an epitome of the Lukan Jesus' good news for the poor. In Thomas, there is no wedding banquet but a simple dinner, and the guests refuse because the invitation conflicts with their business interests. Matthew is unique in allegorizing the punishment of the refusing guests into the destruction of Jerusalem ("burned their city") and adding the expulsion of the man without a wedding garment.

Matthew's interpretation has sadly provided fuel for anti-Semitism throughout the ages. The refusing guests are equated with the Jewish people, who first heard the invitation of Jesus; their refusal brought about the destruction of the Temple. The substitute guests are thought to be Christian converts. Such a view is unfortunately part of the "blame game" in the first century. Josephus, a Jewish historian, wrote the most vivid description of the fall of the Temple and blamed it on the fanaticism of the zealots who did not realize the benefits of Roman rule. Throughout biblical literature and Church history, horrible suffering is often reconciled with God's providential care by viewing suffering as deserved punishment for human sinfulness. After the Shoah (Holocaust) and other horrors of the past century, such a view calls for a radical rethinking of God's nature and the meaning of God's will.

Matthew's addition is a step toward such rethinking. I always feel sorry for the poor guest without the proper attire. On the literal level, it seems absurd that he would have a fine garment after being dragooned in from the streets and main roads. Since clothing can be symbol of new identification with Christ (see Rom 13:14, Gal 3:27; Col 3:12), the wedding garment evokes the good deeds or quality of life that one must show at the time of the great eschatological banquet. Matthew's Christians are not to bask in malicious joy over the destruction of Jerusalem, but to realize that despite their invitation they must be suitably garbed. This is in line with Matthew's "Jewish" theology throughout, where the gifts of God should bear fruit in works of loving kindness and justice.

Many reflections arise from today's readings. Isaiah's beautiful image of God throwing a banquet for people and wiping away every tear, along with the rhythmic cadences of Psalm 23, "The Lord is my shepherd; I shall not want," and "Only goodness and kindness follow me all the days of my life," clash with Matthew's vindictive God, who consigns people to an outer darkness of "wailing and grinding of teeth." This provides an eloquent counter to the old chestnut (still unfortunately heard) that the God of the Old Testament is a God of wrath,while Jesus proclaims a God of mercy. All of us can thank God for the invitation to the eucharistic banquet given in baptism, which is an anticipation of the end-time feasting with God and the saints. Catholics today must also question their willingness all too gleefully to join the "blame game." The ongoing season of shame in the Church has funded this game now vigorously played by all sides and often with a total lack of "goodness and kindness." Unlike the sad man without a proper garment, we still have time, but you never know when the final invitation will come.

PRAYING WITH SCRIPTURE

- Pray quietly and often Psalm 23, thinking of how God's goodness and love have followed you.

- Pray in repentance for those times when you are tempted to rejoice over the suffering of others.

- Check out your wedding garment; it might need sprucing up.

Twenty-Ninth Sunday in Ordinary Time

*Readings: Isa 45:1, 4-6; Ps 96:1, 3, 4-5, 7-8, 9-10; 1 Thess 1:1-5b;
Matt 22:15-21*

> **"For our gospel did not come to you in word alone,
> but also in power and in the Holy Spirit
> and with much conviction" (1 Thess 1:5).**

Tax Time in Autumn!

At times we are tempted to wish that certain sayings of Jesus were
lost or omitted from the Gospels. Jesus' sharp answer to the Pharisees
and Herodians in today's gospel might be one of these: "Repay [ren-
der] to Caesar what belongs to Caesar and to God what belongs to God."
Taken out of context, this line has been used to justify a "two kingdom"
theology, where life is divided into two autonomous realms, the secular
and the religious, or worse, to justify unswerving obedience to secular
authority.

Yet these views are far from Matthew's meaning. The setting is a trap
laid for Jesus by opponents. The precise issue is "paying taxes," not the
autonomy of Caesar in the secular sphere. Taxes were an incendiary
issue during the lifetime of Jesus. The Roman Empire imposed a head
tax on the population of Judea and Samaria, and conducted a census to
enforce it. While Jesus was still young (ca. A.D. 6), Judas the Galilean led
a revolt against the census; this uprising was ruthlessly repressed by
the Romans (Acts 5:37-38). The Pharisees, who resented the Roman oc-
cupation of the pure land of Israel, were against the tax, while the Herodians supported it. They are setting a trap for Jesus. He is faced with
being a collaborator or an insurrectionist.

With Solomonic sagacity seasoned with irony, Jesus traps the trappers.
He asks for a coin, which "they" give him. Roman coins contained the
image of the emperor on one side—at this time the infamous Tiberius—
with the inscription "Tiberius Caesar, son of the divine Augustus," and
on the other, the abbreviation of him as "Pontifex Maximus" (high

priest). Since Matthew locates these conflicts with Jewish authorities in the Temple area, the questioners are discredited by carrying the image of a pagan emperor into the Temple.

By responding "Repay to Caesar what belongs to Caesar," Jesus addresses only the census tax and embodies his rejection of violence as a way of dealing with oppressive situations. The second half of the saying, "and to God what belongs to God," is comprehensive and includes all areas of life. The three disputes of Jesus in Matthew 22 culminate in the greatest commandments: loving God with one's whole heart, mind, and soul, and loving one's neighbor as one's self (next Sunday's gospel). Humans, not coins, bear God's true image, and no edict of Caesar can absolve Jesus' followers from this mandate to love God and to see God in the neighbor.

In every age Christians are faced with balancing the demands of Caesar with the commands of God. Catholics in the United States, as an immigrant and often suspect population, had a history of showing that they were "super Americans," more loyal than any group and unwilling to speak out against the government. In recent decades there has been a subtle shift as theologians and bishops questioned governmental stands on the issues of war and capital punishment. On September 17, 2002, Bishop Wilton Gregory, president of the United States Conference of Catholic Bishops, wrote a letter to President Bush raising questions about the justice of a preemptive attack on Iran. Sadly, though, the prophetic voice of the bishops is one of the victims of the recent season of shame and sorrow.

Bishop Gregory's statement was given only cursory notice by the media, and the consistent ethic of life was a casualty of the Dallas meeting. Governor Frank Keating of Oklahoma, whom the bishops chose to monitor their compliance with the charter on protection of children and young people, was an uncompromising supporter of the death penalty, quite in contrast to the recent statements of Pope John Paul II (*Gospel of Life*, no. 56) and the revised edition of the Catechism of the Catholic Church. Though Governor Keating, at the urging of significant bishops, later resigned after comparing the bishops to mafia hoods, his opposition to papal teaching did not preclude his initial appointment. The seamless garment of a consistent ethic of life lay in tatters on the floor of a Dallas hotel.

In coming months and years Catholics may be called on more and more to think about just what they should render to Caesar and to recall that all Caesars and "messiahs" are subordinate to God's will. Paul summons his community at Thessalonica to preserve and grow in the "work of faith and labor of love and endurance in hope." What better way is there to repay to God what is truly God's?

PRAYING WITH SCRIPTURE

- Pray for world leaders that they realize what they must "render" to God.

- Pray in gratitude for those who speak out against the encroachments of Caesar.

- Imitate Jesus in rejecting violence as a way to resolve conflict.

Thirtieth Sunday in Ordinary Time

Readings: Exod 22:20-26; Ps 18:2-3, 3-4, 47, 51; 1 Thess 1:5c-10; Matt 22:34-40

"I love you, O Lord, my strength" (Ps 18:2).

BACK TO BASICS!

Just for fun, with the help of the search engine Google, I did a web search on the word "love" and found at least 54,700,000 sites, thankfully well ahead of "hate" with 6,400,000 hits. "All You Need Is Love" was a stunning Beatles' hit in 1967, and the Centrum Silver set is lulled by Perry Como's "Love Makes the World Go Round." In today's gospel Jesus tells us that "the whole law and the prophets" depend on the commands to love God "with all your heart, with all your soul, and with all your mind" and "your neighbor as yourself." Today's readings make a fine prelude to the coming celebrations of All Saints and All Souls, which herald again those who truly loved God and neighbor.

In hearing Jesus' word we are listening to the voice of Jesus the Jewish teacher, since he cites texts from Deuteronomy 6:5 and Leviticus 19:18. Nor is Jesus unique in summarizing the law by two central commands. The great rabbi Hillel, when challenged to recite the whole Torah standing on one foot, replied, "What you hate for yourself, do not do to your neighbor. This is the whole law. The rest is commentary" (*Babylonian Talmud*). The first-century Jewish teacher Philo affirmed that love of God and love of neighbor fulfill the whole law. Loving the neighbor as oneself does not mean that love of others cannot exist without healthy love of self, but that one must place oneself in the situation of the neighbor, as illustrated by the reading from Exodus.

While exhortations to love the neighbor reappear frequently in the New Testament, surprisingly there are few commands to love God. A command to love God seems puzzling and difficult, for if love is spontaneous and free, how can it be commanded? God does not really need our service, nor is God changed by our love as is a neighbor or a loved

126

one. God is also absolute mystery, and it is difficult to really love what we do not know. Often the command to love God is collapsed into service of neighbor. Christians are much more at ease speaking of following God's will, serving God, or praying to God in hope and faith.

Profound human love for another offers an image of love of God. I have watched people after fifty or sixty years of marriage content to sit quietly in each other's presence, yet become quickly upset if the spouse returns home later than expected, even when absent for only little more than an hour. Behind such silent presence lie decades of knowledge, care, and trials borne together. It is also an act of gratitude for years of mutual commitment. Love of God is like this. Often it is best expressed in simply sitting and quietly realizing how God has been a partner in every aspect of life. Biblical love of God is gratitude and remembrance for what God has done rather than a project of what we do for God. Hymns of praise and thanksgiving permeate the psalms, and great figures of biblical thought are called "friends of God." The Beatles had it right—"All You Need Is Love."

PRAYING WITH SCRIPTURE

- Sitting quietly, speak words of love to God.

- Pray quietly the words of Hillel.

- Gratefully think of people who have been "sacraments" of God's love in your life.

Thirty-First Sunday in Ordinary Time

Readings: Mal 1:14b–2:2b, 8-10; Ps 131:1, 2, 3; 1 Thess 2:7b-9, 13; Matt 23:1-12

> **"The greatest among you must be your servant"**
> **(Matt 23:11).**

JOB DESCRIPTION FOR CHURCH LEADERS!

As the liturgical year winds down, the Church is less concerned with the number of shopping days until Christmas than with sobering reflections on the end of all days. The Gospels conclude with Jesus' final instructions to his disciples, his final testaments, which weave together words of hope and warnings about the pitfalls that loom during his absence.

Today's gospel launches a bitter polemic against the Pharisees, which is almost a caricature of the historical Pharisees. Its purpose is less to pillory them than to warn the leaders of Matthew's community about certain "pharisaical" attitudes. They preach, but do not practice; they lay burdens on people without lifting a finger to lighten them; they revel in external signs of respect and honor—elegant garments, privileged places at worship and at banquets, concern for official titles. In contrast, Jesus' disciples are to be equal brothers and sisters with only one Father in heaven, and one master, Christ, while their chosen title should be servant, ones who seeks humiliation rather than exaltation.

When coupled with Malachi's attack on the priests who cause many to falter and show partiality, the gospel sounds a strong warning to religious leaders of all ages. Matthew has long been the bulwark of ecclesiastical leadership, with the Petrine promise of 16:15-18 serving as a "gospel within a gospel." Yet, reading it through the lens of the institutional leadership dilutes its message. From Jesus' first great sermon, in which he praises the poor in spirit, the meek and humble, the mournful and merciful, and those who seek peace and justice, until his final proclamation that he is hidden in the least of his brothers and sisters, he heralds values directly opposed to dominating power. Rather than laying burdens on people without lifting a finger, Matthew's Jesus will give rest to those who "labor and are burdened" (11:28), and his prime "honorific title" is "glutton and drunkard, friend of tax collectors and sinners" (11:19).

In today's gospel Jesus summons his disciples to be a contrast society free of the pretensions of power and office. John P. Meier, a premier Catholic New Testament scholar, comments that in chapter 23 "Matthew is obviously concerned about a type of nascent 'clericalism' that is threatening his church," and "may see in all these tendencies the danger that a good and necessary leadership role will turn into domination, monopoly and 'clericalism'"(*Antioch and Rome*, 70–71). More pithily, the curmudgeon and "Sage of Baltimore" H. L. Mencken once described an archbishop as "a Christian ecclesiastic of a rank superior to that attained by Christ."

The Church is not exempt from the bureaucratization that has affected all elements of society, and the higher the ecclesiastical office, the more a bureaucratic model dominates. Though diocesan bishops are faced with almost insurmountable tasks, the Decree on the Pastoral Office of Bishops in the Church issued by Vatican II highlighted their primary role as "spiritual guides to their flock," proclaimers of God's word, and pastors to their priests. When speaking to newly consecrated bishops, Pope John Paul II recalled that during the ordination ceremony, when the priest puts his hands between those of the bishop, it is not simply a one-way gesture of obedience, but "in reality, the gesture commits them both: priest and Bishop. The young priest chooses to entrust himself to the Bishop and, for his part, the Bishop obliges himself to look after those hands." This is a "primary duty" for every diocesan bishop" (Sept. 29, 2002).

Along with a deep commitment to protection of the children, a welcome byproduct of the crisis in the Church beginning in January 2002 could be that Church leaders might feel a new confidence and freedom to pursue what is essential to their office and mission. The meetings and memos may wait; God's good people cannot.

Paul provides a counter-vision to dominating and distant leadership. His care is that of a "nursing mother" for his children; who among them shared not only the "gospel of God, but our very selves as well, so dearly beloved had you become to us." Later Paul writes: "We treated each one of you as a father treats his children, exhorting and encouraging you" (1 Thess 2:11-12). A nursing woman's love and a father's encouragement are wed in Paul's pastoral consciousness. There is a deep lesson here for a Church so characterized by patterns of exclusive male control.

PRAYING WITH SCRIPTURE

- Imitate the psalmist, who trustfully prays to the maternal God "like a weaned child on its mother's lap" (Ps 131:2).

- Pray for Church leaders at a very trying time in their lives.
- Reflect on how the "word of God . . . is now at work in you who believe" (1 Thess 2:13).

November 1

All Saints

Readings: Rev 7:2-4, 9-14; Ps 24:1-2, 3-4, 5-6; 1 John 3:1-3;
Matt 5:1-12a

"See what love the Father has bestowed on us
that we may be called children of God" (1 John 3:1).

WHAT, ME A SAINT?

During the moving memorials of the attacks on September 11, 2001, we gazed upon a collage of the extraordinary goodness of ordinary people. Those who would flinch if called "saints" acted just like them. Today we celebrate such saints throughout the ages, that great cloud of witnesses, whose lives, known to millions or to only a few, became a prism through which shone the multicolored grace and love of God.

Matthew's Beatitudes tell us that such people are happy because they have received the blessings of God. Contrary to the values of the world, God's favor rests upon the poor whose hope looks to him and upon those who quietly mourn and lament a broken world, possess the quiet power and confidence of "the meek," and feel the pangs of hunger and thirst for a world where justice reigns. The first four Beatitudes speak of longing and hope, while the final five bless those who actively seek mercy, peace, integrity of heart expressed in word and deed, and are willing to suffer in the quest for justice.

Matthew also weaves throughout his Gospel a picture of Jesus, who embodies the Beatitudes he proclaims. Jesus exhorts others to be meek and describes himself as meek and humble of heart (11:29). He praises the merciful, and his miracles are acts of mercy (9:13, 27; 12:7); he mourns over the impending fate of Jerusalem (23:37); his disciples are to be emissaries of peace (10:13); he will bring justice to the nations (12:18) and is persecuted for the sake of justice (27:23). The final words of Matthew's Gospel are that he will be with his disciples through all the ages; the saints are the living presence of Christ.

The tradition of canonizing saints has a long history, but it is rooted in the experience of people who recognized saints in their midst. Mother Teresa, now Blessed Mother Teresa, was widely recognized as a saint during her life, and people call others "saints," even if not formally declared so. Perhaps we best make our own little canon of saints, people who have in a special way made the love of God real in our world, who are blessed because God's beauty "is reflected in their faith" (opening prayer). Such people are often hidden among the cranky and the crazy, the gentle and the disturbing, the forgotten and the unforgettable, the joyful and the doleful—and might appear in an occasional glance in the mirror.

PRAYING WITH SCRIPTURE

- In prayer form a canon of "saints" who have embodied God's love and grace.

- Repeat often in prayer the words of 1 John: "We are God's children now."

- What signs of holiness do you see flowering in the Church today?

Thirty-Second Sunday in Ordinary Time

Readings: Wis 6:12-16; Ps 63:2, 3-4, 5-6, 7-8; 1 Thess 4:13-18; Matt 25:1-13

> **"Resplendent and unfading is wisdom, and she is readily perceived by those who love her"**
> **(Wis 6:12).**

GET ME TO THE CHURCH ON TIME!

The coming weeks present a troika of parables that conclude the public teaching of Jesus in Matthew. These constitute his final testament to the disciples, a manual of discipleship for life "between the times"—the time of Jesus' earthly presence and of his triumphant return. They have a menacing tone, in jarring contrast to the voice of one who was meek and humble of heart. Five young women have the door of a feast slammed in their face; a timid and fearful steward is cast into outer darkness, where people will weep and gnash their teeth; and people who were clueless about the presence of Jesus are consigned to eternal punishment.

The story of the wise and foolish virgins, like other parables, is taken from the world of everyday experience. The sad but beautiful film *A Wedding in Galilee* shows that even today a village wedding is a major event. Matthew's parable portrays the return of the wedding party from the bride's home to the groom's home, where the actual marriage ceremony and feast will take place. The bride has ten young women attendants, who will wait and welcome her to the new home with festive lamps to both greet the party and light the way.

The story is relatively simple. Since the wedding party is delayed until midnight, the young women fall asleep, only to be awakened by a loud cry that the procession is near. They all wake up and relight their lamps, when the foolish ones who had brought no oil ask the others to share their oil, only to be met by the harsh reply, "No, for there may not be enough for us and you," and are offered the dubiously helpful suggestion to go and buy some—at midnight, when all shops would be closed! The foolish ones, perhaps doubly so now, go to seek oil. We never know whether they found it, but when they return, the feast has started and the door is barred. They call out, "Lord, Lord," only to have the groom reply harshly, "Amen, I say to you, I do not know you."

There are more interpretations to this parable than there are young women. Many people see it simply as an allegory created by the early Church to urge watchfulness during Jesus' absence. God as the bridegroom, the spouse of Israel, is applied to Jesus in the New Testament (Matt 9:15), and calling the women "virgins" rather than "bridesmaids" reflects the Pauline view of the Church as a virgin espoused to Christ" (2 Cor 11:2). There is also tension between the application "stay awake" and the parable itself, since all the young women sleep. Some readers think that the ones who should have been condemned were the "wise," the somewhat selfish and nasty bridesmaids (Alpha Girls), who would not share their oil. More convincing is that lamps lit and supplied with oil are symbols of the works of love and mercy that one must have at the final judgment. These cannot really be shared with others, so the narrative is a warning against both moral procrastination and presumption.

Surprisingly, commentators rarely focus on the "wise" virgins. The first reading contains a beautiful image of Lady Wisdom (Greek, *sophia*), seeking those who would accept her, "for whoever for her sake keeps vigil shall quickly be free from care." Wisdom is one of the most polyvalent of biblical notions. Wisdom is transcendent knowledge revealed by God and also evokes thoughts of practical know-how along with prudent judgment gained from experience. Wisdom is personified as God's partner in creation, who existed before humanity and now seeks out humanity to respond to her teaching (Prov 8). Five of the bridesmaids are called "wise" (or "prudent") because they carefully assess the needs of the situation and prepare for the future. The lamps are symbols that through their teaching and good deeds they will be lights shining in darkness, which cannot be hidden under a basket. They are guides for the community as it awaits the return of Jesus.

The parable/allegory speaks to us during our long hours of waiting for the bridal party to arrive. The "foolish" bridesmaids warn us against a presumptuous reliance on others, while the wise women are models and guides for Matthew's Church and for ours today. The contemporary Church must be enlightened by women's wisdom. In the gospel the wise are both strong and realistic, and in the first reading Lady Wisdom seeks those worthy of her and "meets them with all solicitude." Yes, the Gospel is ominous: If we do not want to shudder before the words, "I do not know you," there is still time to join the procession behind the "wise virgins."

PRAYING WITH SCRIPTURE

- Prayerfully check the oil supply for your lamps.

- In quiet prayer repeat often Psalm 63:2: "O God, you are my God whom I seek."

- Recall prayerfully and gratefully those whose wisdom was a lamp to your feet.

Thirty-Third Sunday in Ordinary Time

Readings: Prov 31:10-13, 19-20, 30-31; Ps 128:1-2, 3, 4-5;
1 Thess 5:1-6; Matt 25:14-30

> **"Blessed are you who fear the Lord,**
> **who walk in his ways!" (Ps 128:2).**

THE PAROUSIA IS NOT FOR WIMPS

Sister Norice, the sixth-grade teacher, called me out of class and said that the pastor wanted to see me. In fear and trembling, I went over to the church, only to find that a server was needed for an unexpected funeral. After Mass, Monsignor Nelligan gave me two dollars, a huge sum in 1943. Going home on the old, creaky No. 14 streetcar, I checked my pocket every two minutes to make sure the money was still there, and when home, quickly hid it in my secret bank, tucked behind a water heater.

I have always felt a certain sympathy for the battered man who hides his unexpected gift of one talent in the strange parable/allegory presented in today's gospel. Before leaving on a journey, a rich man gives incredible sums to three servants—the first, ten talents; the second five talents; and the third, one talent, which alone equaled the wages of an ordinary worker for twenty years! Without further instructions, the man departs. Hurriedly the first two servants doubled their gifts, while the one-talent man dug a hole and hid his. Upon returning, the master asks what happened to his money. After identical recitations of doubling the gift, the first two are each called "a good and faithful servant" and are placed in charge of even more possessions and welcomed into the joy of the master.

The man with one talent must be despondent and begins immediately with his excuse: "Master, I knew you were a demanding person [lit.: "a hard man"], harvesting where you did not plant and gathering where you did not scatter; so out of fear I went off and buried your talent in the ground." The master's outburst is shocking. He berates the man as wicked and lazy, tells him that he should have invested the

136

money with bankers (contrary to the Jewish laws against usury), gives the talent to the one who already had ten, and exiles the timid servant to the outer darkness to weep and gnash his teeth.

If the master of this parable is to represent the returning Jesus, he seems vindictive, arbitrary, and even somewhat immoral (remember the bankers and the Jewish prohibition of usury!). Is there anything the poor third servant does that explains the bitter response and punishment? Comparison of his excuse with the master's reply gives a clue. He calls the master a "hard" man, who expects returns from his investment and invokes fear as his defense. In replying ("So you knew"), the master admits that he expects a return but never repeats or agrees with the servant, calling him "hard." A person who gives away vast sums (even one talent) may be enterprising but is scarcely hard. The tragic flaw of the one-talent man is that he lived out of fear even when gifted.

Such is the deeper meaning of this allegory. Unlike the waiting virgins of last week's parable, who presumed on the generosity of others, this man is a victim of his own fright. After the predictions of the end time in chapter 24 and the threats of severe judgment awaiting the unfaithful at Jesus' return, Matthew is urging his community not to be timid and fearful, but to take risks. The paradox of biblical revelation is that a merciful, gracious, and compassionate God who liberates us from slavery is also the God who will judge us on the use of our gifts. Every gift of God is also a mandate to bear fruit in God's vineyard.

At first glance the traditional praise of a "worthy wife" from Proverbs seems hardly related to this gospel. Women today may bristle at the overemphasis on household management, but her husband has "entrusted his heart to her." Unlike the one-talent man, she takes this gift and "brings him good and not evil"; she "reaches out her hands to the poor and extends her arms to the needy." She "fears the Lord," which is not the craven fear of the third servant but that love and reverence that spur to action. The liberation of Israel from Egypt begins with the revolt of the midwives, who affirm life in the face of death when they disobey the command to kill the Jewish babies. Therefore, "because the midwives feared God, he built up families for them" (Exod 1:15-21)

The Church in history lives between the times, and some times are worse than others. Today it is easy to let fear govern our lives. A whole political and social culture is nurtured by fear, and it stalks our Church life. Traditionalists fear the gift of Vatican II and a changing Church, and want to keep their treasure intact through a return to dated rituals and arcane theology. Those who welcomed the *aggiornamento* of Pope John XXIII often want to freeze it in time and are fearful of renewing the renewal. The wise women at the wedding feast, the enterprising servants in today's gospel, and the good wife of Proverbs were people of foresight, initiative, and independence. The Church today has been given vast treasures of "talents." Will these increase or remain hidden and guarded?

PRAYING WITH SCRIPTURE

- Prayerfully make an inventory of your gifts and talents

- Ask God to help you to be aware of those fears that can paralyze your life.

- Prayerfully recall times when God praised you for being faithful "in small matters" and welcomed you into the joy of his presence.

The Solemnity of
Our Lord Jesus Christ the King

Readings: Ezek 34:11-12, 15-17; Ps 23:1-2, 2-3, 5-6; 1 Cor 15:20-26, 28;
Matt 25:31-46

"Lord, when did we see you hungry and feed you,
or thirsty and give you drink?" (Matt 25:37).

VIVA CHRISTO REY!

Seventy-eight years ago (November 23, 1927), Father Miguel Pro, S.J., shouted, "Long live Christ the King" moments before he was executed by a firing squad in Mexico City. At age thirty-seven and only two years ordained, he was condemned for ministering to people during a government ban on the Catholic Church. The feast and gospel today herald Jesus as king, but one identified, like Father Pro, with the poor and persecuted, and who himself was executed with the mocking title "King of the Jews."

Two themes resonate through the readings: the shepherding care of God: "As a shepherd tends his flock, when he finds himself among his scattered sheep, so I will tend my sheep" (Ezek 34:11, see Ps 23), and the vision of the end time, when Jesus as King and Son of Man will separate the evildoers from good people as a shepherd separates the sheep from the goats.

Matthew's grand pageant of the Last Judgment has become the "Gospel within the Gospel" for people dedicated to works of charity and justice for today's multitudes suffering hunger, thirst, horrible illness, and imprisonment. Most surprising in this parable is that Jesus is identified with such people and was unknown even to those who ministered to him. A "universalistic" interpretation has become commonplace: Anyone (Christian or non-Christian) who does such works of mercy to another person is doing them to Christ and will be rewarded by Christ.

Many recent commentators are not at ease with the universalistic interpretation. This narrative concludes a long discourse *to disciples* telling them how they are to live during Jesus' absence. When Jesus departs after the resurrection, he commissions his disciples as missionaries to the ends of the earth, baptizing in the name of the Father, Son, and Holy Spirit and spreading his teaching, but always with the consciousness that he would be "with them" until the end of the age (Matt 28:16-20). The setting for the story of the "sheep and the goats" is at the end of the age, when we learn that Jesus was always "with them" among the least of his brothers and sisters. These least are called "brothers," a term that Matthew reserves for disciples of Jesus. The Gentile nations will be judged on how they received Christian disciples, the least of Jesus' brothers and sisters, who carry the presence of the absent Jesus.

Over the years I have vacillated between these two interpretations but have come to favor the "discipleship" interpretation. The least of Jesus' brothers and sisters are disciples, who bear the same kinds of apostolic suffering that Paul speaks of: hunger, thirst, living as a stranger, nakedness, sickness, and imprisonment (1 Cor 4:10-13; 2 Cor 11:23-29). Paul sees these as signs that "the transcendent power belongs to me" (Christ), or "power is made perfect in weakness." Apostolic sufferings hide the power and presence of Christ.

Matthew is not simply concerned about punishing resistant Gentiles. Those Gentiles who ministered to Christ hidden in the missionaries are called just. The horizon of this narrative is apocalyptic. In apocalyptic thought, scenes of judgment disclose the transcendent values that should have been operative prior to the end of history. Apocalyptic is a view of history and human life from God's side. The parable reveals that justice is constituted by acts of loving kindness and mercy to those in need; the world will be made "right" or "just" when the way the least are treated becomes the norm of action. What is done positively *for* them is not to be limited *to* them.

Does all this make a difference to the Church today? The sufferings borne by the least of the brothers and sisters of the Son of Man summon the Church to be an authentic and faithful witness of the gospel. The Church cannot preach acts of loving kindness to the hungry, the thirsty, the imprisoned, and the naked unless it, too, is a Church in mission and bears these same sufferings. No Gospel is harsher than Matthew's on an ethics of words without deeds. The Church today suffers from a massive credibility gap, and the values that it proposes *to* the nations must be those that the Church itself witnesses *in the midst* of the nations.

In recent decades a river of statements on injustice, the dangers of wealth, care for immigrants, concern for the homeless, and a wide variety of human rights issues have flowed forth from powerful statements of Pope John Paul II to local bishops conferences.

Yet, "social justice" is often for external consumption rather than internal assimilation. Concern for social justice seems a marginal qualification among many episcopal appointees. While protesting violation of human rights throughout the world, there has been a progressive retrenchment of such rights within the Church, sadly illustrated by Bernard Häring's statement that though he was tried four times on capital charges by Nazi courts, he would prefer to stand again before a "court of war of Hitler" than before the Congregation for the Doctrine of the Faith (*My Witness for the Church*, pp. 132–133).

Today *Christo Rey* truly reigns among those whose authentic witness reminds us of the demands of justice in the world. These embrace not only the multitude of martyrs for justice, who, like Father Pro, stretched out their arms to death, but a cloud of witnesses at work in homeless shelters and in classrooms, in prison cells and retreat houses, in lobbying for the poor and in confronting the prosperous. They show us what justice means and how Christ reigns in their lives as they guide us "in right paths for his name's sake" (Ps 23:3).

PRAYING WITH SCRIPTURE

- Repeat often the opening prayer: "Open our hearts, free the entire world to rejoice in his peace, to glory in his justice, to live in his love."

- Pray that the reign of Christ may supplant the reign of hatred and violence.

- As Advent approaches, pray how individuals, families, and communities may witness to today's gospel.

Select Annotated Bibliography
on the Gospel of Matthew

COMMENTARIES

Garland, David. *Reading Matthew: A Literary and Theological Commentary on the First Gospel.* New York: Crossroad, 1993. A good popular commentary.

Hare, Douglas. *Matthew.* Interpretation Bible Commentary. Louisville: Westminster/Knox, 1993. A good commentary in a series oriented to the "religious professional."

Harrington, Daniel. *The Gospel According to Matthew.* Collegeville Bible Commentary. Collegeville: Liturgical Press, 1982. This is one of the volumes in the immensely helpful series of books that give the biblical text and excellent commentary. The commentary to the whole series is available in one volume as the *Collegeville Bible Commentary.*

———. *Matthew.* Sacra Pagina. Collegeville: Liturgical Press, 1991. An excellent commentary at the level of the "religious professional."

McKenzie, Alice M. *Matthew.* Interpretation Bible Study. Louisville: Westminster/Knox, 1998. Designed for adults and older youth, Interpretation Bible Studies can be used in small groups, in church/school classes, in large group presentations.

Meier, J. *Matthew.* New Testament Message 3. Wilmington: Glazier, 1980. A very insightful commentary in English on Matthew.

Senior, Donald. *The Gospel of Matthew.* Interpreting Biblical Texts Series. Nashville: Abingdon, 1997. Senior has been writing on Matthew for three decades and has condensed much scholarship into this very readable commentary.

Smith, R. H. *Matthew.* Minneapolis: Augsburg, 1989. An excellent popular commentary.

Witherup, Ronald D., s.s. *Matthew: God with Us: Spiritual Commentaries.* Hyde Park, N.Y.: New City Press, 2000. One of the best commentaries available for priest and parishioners.

GENERAL WORKS ON MATTHEW

Aune, David. The *Gospel of Matthew in Current Study.* Grand Rapids: Eerdmans, 2001.

Brown, R. E. *The Churches the Apostles Left Behind.* New York/Ramsey: Paulist Press, 1984. The chapter on Matthew is an interesting view of the community of Matthew with relevance to contemporary Church.

Kingsbury, J. D. *Matthew as Story*. 2nd ed. Minneapolis, Minn.: Fortress Press, 1988. A good literary reading of the Gospel.

———. *Matthew*. Proclamation Commentaries. Philadelphia: Fortress, 1977. An outstanding presentation of Matthew's theology.

Luz, Ulrich. *Matthew in History: Interpretation Influence, and Effects*. Minneapolis: Fortress, 1994. A notable study of the impact of Matthew.

———. *The Theology of the Gospel of Matthew*. Cambridge: Cambridge University Press, 1995. One of the very best short presentations of Matthew's theology.

Meier, John P. *The Vision of Matthew: Christ, Church and Morality in the First Gospel*. New York: Paulist Press, 1979. A superb series of essays in commentary style.

Powell, Mark Alan. *God with Us: A Pastoral Theology of Matthew's Gospel*. Minneapolis: Fortress Press, 1995. Approaches the material, not from perspective of traditional "theological" categories, but from pastoral ones, e.g., Mission, Stewardship, Social Justice.

Saldarini, Anthony. *Matthew's Christian-Jewish Community*. Chicago: University of Chicago Press, 1994. A scholarly but very readable study that provides a wealth of information on Matthew and Judaism.

Senior, D. *"What Are They Saying About Matthew?"* Rev. ed. New York/Ramsey: Paulist Press, 1996. A first-rate survey of the present state of scholarship on Matthew. Highly recommended for teachers.

Soares-Prabhu, George. *The Dharma of Jesus*. Ed. Francis Xavier D'Sa. Maryknoll, N.Y.: Orbis Books, 2003. A collection of essays by the late Indian Jesuit, who integrates non-Western thought with original exegesis.

Thompson, W. G. *Matthew's Story: Good News for Uncertain Times*. Mahwah, N.J.: Paulist Press, 1989. A reading of Matthew for contemporary spirituality, with special stress on the use of Matthew for prayer.